ADORATION
prayer book

Bob Hartley

TABLE
OF CONTENTS

Message from Bob Hartley

In 1983, I had asked the Lord over and over what was on His heart, what was He thinking and feeling, what were His desires and dreams, and what He showed me has captured my heart ever since! He showed me cities and nations and how He desired that they would love Him well and hope in Him. After this, He showed me 50 million "Hope Bringers" who were called to bring the wisdom and hope of who God is into cities and nations. They would declare God's 'better than' plans that would unlock the Kingdom of God over entire geographic regions. The Lord reminded me of Deuteronomy 7:17, where He asked the children of Israel, "If you should say in your heart, 'These nations are greater than I; how can I dispossess them?' I saw that these "Hope Bringers" had confidence that God was greater than the nations, like the 2 spies in Numbers 13!

These "Hope Bringers" were being invited into a royal journey with Jesus that would establish their hearts in unshakable hope in God that would bring transformation into every arena of life. These "Hope Bringers" were from every station and walk of life; they were mothers, business people, church leaders, artists, politicians, educators, students and laborers. They brought hope through continual adoration of God, like David who magnified the Lord seven times a day!

Adoration is our golden key, magnifying God all throughout the day. This prayer manual of hope truly is a golden treasure that can help to unlock the power of adoration in your life!

The Golden Treasure of Hope in Prayer

The Lord revealed to me through Bob Jones, a prophetic mentor and friend, that I (with others), was to help unlock hope in God, which is a golden treasure that has been buried for thousands of years, as in Isaiah 45:3, "I will give you the treasures of darkness and hidden wealth of secret places, so that you may know that it is I, the LORD, the God of Israel, who calls you by your name." The Lord told me that through devotion, I would become "Hartley the Heart" and that I, with others, would help to uncover the God of Hope to defeat the Idol of Despair that is so prevalent in our day.

The Journey of Hope

The Lord began to show me a holy progression into His presence called the Journey of Hope. He was calling these 50 million "Hope Bringers" to walk out this biblical journey like Song of Solomon 1–8. This reveals how we are to build a life of hoping in God for every area and every season of life. He showed me that this journey is all about discovering the God of Hope in deeper ways and growing in intimacy with Him. It is about thriving in this life, not just surviving until He returns! He came to give us life and He brings us life more abundant and it is available today!

The Hope Room

Many years ago, I began the first step on this journey, which is the Hope Room, or the Adoration Room experience where Face to Face Prayer happens, like the disciples being invited to the upper room and entering that place of devotion and adoring Jesus. When they saw Him in a new way, everything changed! They gained an unshakable Hope in God in that place. I discovered that this journey is not a method or program, but meeting with the One you love. It's all about relationship with the man Christ Jesus. I found that adoration prayer is the first and "always" step on the journey, it is the foundation to the kingdom!

Psalm 34:3– "O magnify the Lord with me, and let us exalt His name together."

So I began to spend hours a day in adoration while cleaning theaters, I would spend time with him in my car, driving through the city and talking to Him, I would write poems and I would sing Him songs. I adored Him and the wonder of who He is, like Psalm 100.

Psalm 100:1,4–5- "Shout joyfully to the Lord, all the earth. Serve the Lord with gladness; come before Him with joyful singing. .. Enter His gates with thanksgiving and His courts with praise. Give thanks to Him, bless His name. For the Lord is good; His loving–kindness is everlasting and His faithfulness to all generations.

Definition
of Adoration (face to face prayer)

A. From Webster's
   1. To honor and admire profoundly and respectfully, implying love and stressing the notion of an individual and personal attachment.
   2. To worship or honor as a deity or as divine
   3. To show devoted deferential honor to : regard as worthy of great honor
   4. Synonyms: revere, reverence, venerate, worship,

B. To adore is to give our entire devotion. It is not about making requests of Him, but giving Him our whole heart and all of our affection.

C. To adore Him is to love Him more than gold and silver. To adore Him is to love Him more than all of the pleasures this world has to offer.
   1. SOS 1:2 – "…for your love is better than wine"
   2. Phil 3:8 – "More than that, I count all things to be loss in view of the surpassing value of knowing Christ Jesus my Lord, for whom I have suffered the loss of all things, and count them but rubbish so that I may gain Christ."

D. To adore is to appreciate and value Him for who He is and to give Him the love He is due in all arenas and seasons of life. To adore is to give Him honor and receive His love.
   1. 1 Corinthians 7:35 – "I am saying this for your own good, not to restrict you, but that you may live in a right way in undivided devotion to the Lord."

E. To adore Him is to focus on Him appropriately with faith in who He is. To adore Him is to see that He is more than enough, and that every obstacle and challenge of life is an opportunity for encounter with Him!
   1. Colossians 1:15–20 – "He is the image of the invisible God, the firstborn over all creation. For by Him all things were created: things in heaven and on earth, visible and invisible, whether thrones or powers or rulers or authorities; all things were created by Him and for Him. He is before all things, and in Him all things hold together. And He is the head of the body, the church; He is the beginning and the firstborn from among the dead, so that in everything He might have the supremacy. For God was pleased to have all His fullness dwell in Him, and through Him to reconcile to Himself all things, whether things on earth or things in heaven, by making peace through His blood, shed on the cross."

F. To adore Him is to look into His eyes. It is not talking about Him or around Him but TO Him. It is a living relationship with the Son of Man. To adore Him is to behold Him in all His glory.
   1. SOS 5:12 – "His eyes are like doves beside streams of water, bathed in milk, sitting beside a full pool." We adore Him to see our friend, His face and His eyes. When we do, everything changes!
   2. Matthew 26:7, 13 – "A woman came to Him with an alabaster jar of very expensive perfume, which she poured on His head as He was reclining at the table…' I tell you the truth, wherever this gospel is preached throughout the world, what she has done will also be told, in memory of her.'" When we adore Him, as this woman did, everywhere we go, the atmosphere is changed. This woman's devotion was spoken of for generations.

G. To adore is to exalt His loveliness, which has great power.
   1. Isaiah 4:2 – In that day the Branch of the LORD will be beautiful and glorious…
   2. Isaiah 28:5 – In that day the LORD of hosts will become a beautiful crown and a glorious diadem to the remnant of His people;

Introduction to Adoration:

A. Adoration or "Face to Face" prayer is loving and magnifying the Lord above all else and in every circumstance and season of life. It is setting our eyes on the prize of knowing Christ Jesus and delighting in who He is. A person in love can do anything! Adoration is about falling in love with Him and giving Him the love He is due!

B. All of life is an opportunity to see and love Him more. We start with a 'Narrow View of God' and through adoration, we move to a 'Broader and Broader and Deeper View' of God,
    1. Like Song of Solomon 1:3–4 to Song of Solomon 3:2 –As we take time to adore in our devotional life, not trying to rush into His presence, but simply loving and delighting in Him, we will cultivate the intimacy we need with Him in all of life.
    2. The most exhilarated person is not the one who has a million dollars, but is the one that experiences God and the reflection of Him in all of life. Adoration takes us to that place!

C. Personal Example of Adoration: Story of My Dad at Christmas
    When I was a child, the kids in my family would give my father gag gifts for Christmas. We would take turns presenting silly poems or witty criticism to him. My siblings were all very bright and could be quite entertaining. My dad always played along with this tradition in good fun.

    One year, however, the routine changed. My oldest sister began to read her poem, but for some reason she couldn't continue. She crumpled the paper she held in her hand, threw it to the floor and looked my dad in the eyes. "Dad, I have never met a man like you. You are as gentle a man I have ever known. You are so honorable and kind."

    My brother picked up where she left off, "Yeah, Dad. You never get worried and burdened, you always turn hard things into joyful things." Another sister shared, "When I get married, Dad, I want to marry a man like you." The next brother began, "Dad, you are unpretentious, you never pretend. You are so sincere and I want to grow up to be a man like you."

    I tucked myself behind the Christmas tree and cried. I loved to see my father loved, hoped in, believed in, and appreciated, as he had done for us countless times! It so moved my heart to see my father's heart cared for and valued in that way.

    That Christmas, I learned firsthand about the power of adoration. I saw how this love and affection made my father feel valued and loved, and how my heart came alive as his heart was cared for in an appropriate way. I realized that our Father in Heaven desires our love and affection as His sons and daughters, and my heart was moved to see Him adored this way.

D. Scriptures about Adoration and Magnifying the Lord
    1. Psalm 22:3 "Yet You are holy, O You who are enthroned upon the praises of Israel."
        A. The Lord sits enthroned on our praises! As we come into agreement with His Kingship, we release His power and authority in the earth realm! He has given authority of the earth to the sons of man, and we have the great privilege to usher in His dominion through our worship and agreement with Him.
    2. Psalm 60:30–31 "I will praise the name of God with song and magnify Him with thanksgiving. And it will please the LORD better than an ox or a young bull with horns and hoofs."
        A. God desires our affection first and foremost, the first commandment is to love the Lord our God with all of our heart, mind, soul and strength! This is more important than our sacrifices or what we can do for Him. He is after our love!
    3. Revelation 7:12 "Amen, blessing and glory and wisdom and thanksgiving and honor and power and might, {be} to our God forever and ever. Amen."
        A. Adoration is the pattern we see in heaven! The Lord is surrounded by worship and adoration continually throughout all of eternity. When we come into agreement with heaven, we release that glory and majesty into our surroundings on earth…"on earth as it is in heaven!"

Application
of Adoration (face to face prayer)

The Power of Face to Face Prayer or Adoration

I began to discover such power coming forth from my inner man through this journey into adoration and devotion prayer. This type of prayer, adoring and magnifying the Lord began to release oil for my weariness and it opened the door for the rain of the Spirit, which came to refresh, restore and to anoint my body, soul and spirit. In this place of the rain, I became soaked in the presence of God and soaked in His promises for me.

This is the power of adoration! When we abide in this place of devotion to the Lord, we become Adoration Pillars, those who have been rained on by the presence of God, and can then rain on others. We become so soaked in the rain of God that we become aromas and Presence Carriers of Him. The Hope Room is all about the rain! As we magnify and adore the Lord, He sends His rain of refreshment over us! As we adore and magnify who God is over others, His presence washes over them and brings healing and refreshment.

The Hope Prayer Manual

This manual is an advanced tool to guide you into adoration prayer. It is very simple to use and is formatted so that you can cultivate your own love language with God. Use it to proclaim His different faces as they relate to particular arenas and seasons of your life. The following pages contain suggestions of which faces of God to explore based on our experiences within the different arenas of life.

At the Hartley Institute we have 4 specific faces of God that we focus on each morning during our staff prayer times that we believe the Lord is highlighting to the body of Christ for this season: the Redeemer God, the Supplier God, the Builder God and the Wise God.

Other examples of Marketplace Faces of God to cultivate:
- The Nurturing God who always provides and protects in the midst of the marketplace.
- The Joyful God who causes work to be a fruitful endeavor versus a dutiful burden.
- The "Better than" God who always has a wiser blueprint and an easier yoke.
- The Patriarchal God who builds out for generations to come in all arenas of life.

Suggested Use of this Manual

Begin with 15 minutes a day, and one letter of the alphabet, and begin to declare and adore the different faces of God. Apply the examples from scripture and also your own personal examples within your everyday life situations to take you to a place where you can really taste, touch, and feel the faces of God. Don't stop with what is written! Engage your heart and mind, and dive deep into the beauty of God, creating your own love language and dialogue with God!

Try this with your family. Have your children proclaim the many faces of God and watch how much power comes from adoring the Lord in this way. Try this in your workplaces at your morning staff meetings. Proclaim the faces of God in your specific areas of work. Try this in your schools and universities to form a knowledge of literature and understanding like the young men in Daniel 1:17.

I hope you will find this Hope Prayer Manual deeply enriching. I pray that you will continue this intimate journey of hope, deepening your discovery of the man Christ Jesus.

Next Steps on the Journey of Hope

A. Adoration is the first step on the Journey of Hope. We never leave this place of simple devotion to Christ, but we do add more tools to our tool belt! We continue along the Journey into Confession, Thanksgiving and Supplication Prayer. I've included a brief summary of these steps of the journey below. Look for additional resources for these steps of the Journey, including a Hope Prayer Manuel for each step, as you continue walking with us on this ancient path laid out in the scriptures:

　　1. Jeremiah 6:16– This is what the LORD says: "Stand at the crossroads and look; ask for the ancient paths, ask where the good way is, and walk in it, and you will find rest for your souls…"

B. Confession Prayer is the second step on the Journey of Hope. At this stage of the Journey, as we've adored Him, we now enter into the "God of Life" Room, where we discover the God who is alive and active and to be discovered in all arenas of life: business, government, church, education, family, the marketplace, media and the arts.

　　1. We then apply Confession Prayer, where we confess the nature of God in and through us! We confess His nature in others, and we confess His nature in our circumstances and promises. We don't go above or around the issues and circumstances of the day; with confession prayer, we go right through them, holding the hand of our "Greater than" God!

C. Thanksgiving Prayer is the third step on the Journey of Hope. At this stage, as we've learned to adore and magnify Him first, in Adoration Prayer, and then we've learned how to encounter Him all throughout the day in Confession Prayer, now we come before His Counsel Table, where we are invited to hear His voice on a new level. At His Counsel Table, He gives us the right questions to ask Him, to arrive at the right hopeful solutions for the day.

　　1. We then apply Thanksgiving Prayer, where we position our hearts in thanksgiving and praise for all the ways we have seen Him come through in our daily lives. As we bring to remembrance the mighty acts of the Lord, we have confidence and faith that He will continue to move and act on our behalf in the future, positioning our hearts for a new level of kingdom hearing.

D. Supplication Prayer is the fourth step on the Journey of Hope. At this stage, we have heard His voice clearly at His Counsel Table, now we begin to proclaim with God for our businesses, families, cities and nations in agreement with His heart.

　　1. We then apply Supplication Prayer, where we agree with what we have heard at His Counsel Table. Such faith comes forth from this place that the Job 22:8 reality happens, where we decree a thing and it happens!

For more on Adoration & The Journey of Hope, check out these resources:

"The Hope Journey" Book: Brand New!!
Do you want to learn more about this message of Hope, and how to live a life of confident expectation in the goodness of God? This brand new book, written by Bob Hartley and his daughter Amyann, is a heartfelt account of Bob's own journey into discovery of the Man of Hope Himself. Filled with gripping stories and wisdom from a life lived for Jesus, this book will inspire you to press forward to the high prize of knowing this God of all hope!

"52 Weeks of Hope"
Each week, Bob Hartley and the Deeper Waters team have recorded special "fireside chats" where Bob and others share the most important keys for living an abundant life in God with a living hope for today! Receive one-on-one mentoring from Bob and the Deeper Waters team. This weekly 10 minute video clip is sent directly to your email, and includes practical building blocks to apply to your week, as you embark on this journey of hope! Sign up at 52weeksofhope.com

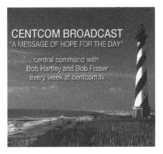

"Centcom Broadcast" every Tuesday night
Don't miss our weekly "Hope Broadcast" on Centcom.tv that gives great practical building blocks and insight into the heart of God for the present hour in the Body of Christ. Free Broadcast every Tuesday night at 7pm, and archived for the remainder of the week; a fresh teaching on how to live as a Hope Bringer and impact your family, business, city and nation with the life–changing force of Hope in God!

"Hope Prayer" CD's
This Hope prayer CD series, features Bob Hartley modeling adoration with the 4 Forgotten Faces of God to be discovered in 2009–2011. Each CD models one of these faces, the Redeemer God, the Supplier God, the Builder God and the Wise God. We encourage you to buy the set of 4 for a great discount, and build your love language with the Lord, unlocking these faces of God in your business, family and everyday life.

"The Hope Kit"

This Hope Kit includes the best Hope feedings to launch you into your journey of hope! This kit includes:

- The Hope DVD Series (an 8 DVD set)
- New Adoration Prayer Book
- The Hope Journey book
- Four Prayer CD's (Face of God as Redeemer, Supplier, Builder and the Wise God)

"Heart of Adoration" CD

For years, Bob Hartley has drawn people into greater intimacy with Jesus through his prayers of Adoration. Now, in the 'Prayers of Adoration' series, these prayers are captured for you, making it easy to add a fresh spark of intimacy to your own personal prayer life. 'Heart of Adoration' focuses on 'Why We Adore God'. These prayers, coupled with instrumental music, provide an inspiring tool that will carry you into the heart of a passionate pursuing God.

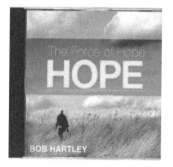

"Jesus Man of Hope" Prayer CD

This CD in the Hope prayer CD series, features Bob Hartley adoring Jesus the Man of Hope, and how He hoped in His Father, how He hoped in people and called out the greatness in them, how He hoped in the next generation, and how He hoped in cities and nations. This is a powerful tool of devotion that will strengthen your love language with God and bring you into face–to–face encounter with Jesus the man of hope.

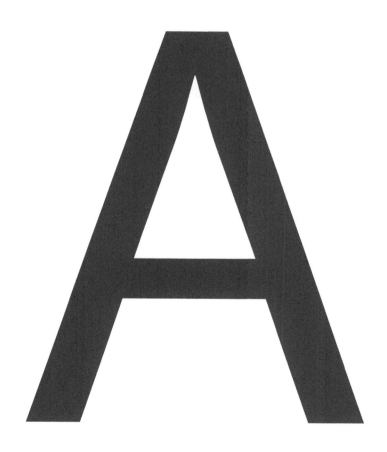

You are the God who is ABUNDANTLY AVAILABLE.

"God is our refuge and strength and abundantly available help in time of need." –Psalm 46:1 (Amp)

My Personal Experience:

You are the God who is APPROACHABLE by all.

"Come near to God and He will come near to you..." –James 4:8

"Let us then approach the throne of grace with confidence, so that we may receive mercy and find grace to help us in our time of need." –Hebrews 4:16

"Then Abraham approached him and said: "Will you sweep away the righteous with the wicked?" –Genesis 18:23 (Amp)

"Suffer the little children to come to me." —Matthew 14:14

"This is the confidence we have in approaching that if we ask according to His will, He hears us." —1 John 5:14

My Personal Experience:

You are the God who is ATTENTIVE to my prayers.

"Now My eyes will be open and My ears attentive to the prayers offered in this place." –2 Chronicles 7:15

"The eyes of the LORD are on the righteous and His ears are attentive to their cry..." –Psalm 34:15

"For the eyes of the Lord are on the righteous and His ears are attentive to their prayer." —1 Peter 3:12

My Personal Experience:

You are the God who ANSWERS me.

"To the LORD I cry aloud, and He answers me from His holy hill. Selah." –Psalm 3:4

"Now I know that the LORD saves His anointed; He answers him from His holy heaven with the saving power of His right hand." –Psalm 20:6

"I call on the Lord in my distress and He answers me." —Psalm 120:1

My Personal Experience:

You are the ACCEPTING God who accepts me.

"He who receives and welcomes and accepts you receives and welcomes and accepts Me," –Matthew. 10:40 (Amp)

"Then Peter began to speak: "I now realize how true it is that God does not show favoritism but accepts men from every nation who fear him and do what is right." –Acts 10:34–35

"It was to demonstrate and prove at the present time (in the now season) that He Himself is righteous and that He justifies and accepts as righteous him who has [true] faith in Jesus." –Romans 3:26

"Accept one another, just as Christ accepted you, in order to bring praise to God." —Romans 15:7

My Personal Experience:

You are the AWESOME God.

"Who among the gods is like You, O LORD? Who is like You– majestic in holiness, awesome in glory, working wonders?" –Exodus 15:11 (Amp)

"Do not be terrified by them, for the LORD your God, Who is among you, is a great and awesome God." –Deuteronomy 7:21 (Amp)

"Lord, the great and awesome God, who keeps His covenant of love with all who love Him and obey His commands." —Daniel 9:4

"He is more awesome than all who surround Him." —Psalm 89:7

"Come and see what God has done. How awesome His works in man's behalf." —Psalm 66:5

My Personal Experience:

You are the ALMIGHTY God.

"And God said to him, "I am God Almighty…." –Genesis 35:11

"Who is He, this King of glory? The LORD Almighty– He is the King of glory. Selah" –Psalm 24:10

"I am the Alpha and the Omega," says the Lord God, "who is, and who was, and who is to come, the Almighty." —Revelation 1:8

My Personal Experience:

You are God ABOUNDING in love.

"And he passed in front of Moses, proclaiming, "The LORD, the LORD, the compassionate and gracious God, slow to anger, abounding in love and faithfulness…" –Exodus 34:6 (Amp)

"Return to the LORD your God, for he is gracious and compassionate, slow to anger and abounding in love," –Joel 2:13 (Amp)

"You, O Lord are a compassionate and gracious God, slow to anger, abounding in love and faithfulness." —Psalm 86:15

My Personal Experience:

You are the ADVOCATE.

"Even now my witness is in heaven; my advocate is on high." –Job 16:19

"And I will ask the Father, and He will give you another Comforter (Counselor, Helper, Intercessor, Advocate, Strengthener, and Standby), that He may remain with you forever–" –John 14:16 (Amp)

"My dear children, I write this to you so that you will not sin. But if anybody does sin, we have one who speaks to the Father in our defense—Jesus Christ, the Righteous One."—1 John 2:1

My Personal Experience:

You are the AVENGER.

"He is the God who avenges me, who puts the nations under me…" –2 Samuel 22:48 (Amp)

"O LORD, the God who avenges, O God who avenges, shine forth." –Psalm 94:1

"He is the God who avenges me, who subdues nations under me, who saves me from my enemies." —Psalm 18:47

My Personal Experience:

You are ALPHA and Omega.

"I am the Alpha and the Omega," says the Lord God, "Who is, and Who was, and Who is to come, the Almighty." –Revelation 1:8

"He said to me: 'It is done. I am the Alpha and the Omega, the Beginning and the End. To him who is thirsty I will give to drink without cost from the spring of the water of life'." –Revelation 21:6

"I am the Alpha and the Omega, the First and the Last, the Beginning and the End" –Revelation 22:13

I am the Alpha and Omega." —Revelations 1:8

My Personal Experience:

You are the God who is ACTIVE on my behalf.

"Jesus said to them, 'My Father is always at His work to this very day, and I, too, am working.'" –John 5:17

"For the word of God is living and active. Sharper than any double–edged sword, it penetrates even to dividing soul and spirit, joints and marrow; it judges the thoughts and attitudes of the heart." –Hebrews 4:12

"For from of old no one has heard nor perceived by the ear, nor has the eye seen a God besides You, Who works and shows Himself active on behalf of him who [earnestly] waits for Him." –Isaiah 64:4 (Amp)

My Personal Experience:

You are ABBA, our Father.

"For you did not receive a spirit that makes you a slave again to fear, but you received the Spirit of sonship. And by Him we cry, "Abba, Father." –Romans 8:15 (Amp)

"Because you are sons, God sent the Spirit of His Son into our hearts, the Spirit who calls out, "Abba, Father." –Galatians 4:6 (Amp)

"And He said Abba Father, all things are possible for you." —Mark 14:36

My Personal Experience:

You are the ANOINTED one.

"The Spirit of the Sovereign LORD is on me, because the LORD has anointed me to preach good news to the poor. He has sent me to bind up the brokenhearted, to proclaim freedom for the captives and release from darkness for the prisoners," –Isaiah 61:1

"How God anointed Jesus of Nazareth with the Holy Spirit and power, and how he went around doing good and healing all who were under the power of the devil, because God was with him." –Acts 10:38

"You are the most excellent of men and Your lips have been anointed with grace, since God has blessed You forever." –Psalm 45:2

"The kings of the earth take their stand and the rulers gather together against the LORD and against his Anointed One." —Psalm 2:2

My Personal Experience:

You are the Lord who ARMS ME.

"It is God who arms me with strength and makes my way perfect." –Psalm 18:32

My Personal Experience:

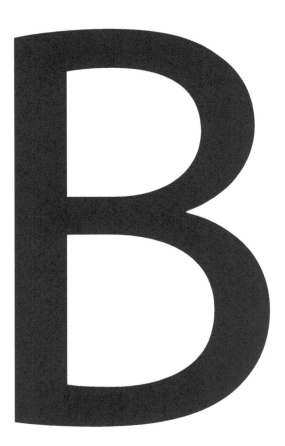

You are the BEAUTIFUL God

"He has made everything beautiful in its time." –Ecclesiastes 3:11

"In that day the Branch of the LORD will be beautiful and glorious, and the fruit of the land will be the pride and glory of the survivors in Israel." –Isaiah 4:2

"In that day the LORD Almighty will be a glorious crown, a beautiful wreath for the remnant of His people." –Isaiah 28:5

"… So did You lead Your people [Lord] to make for Yourself a beautiful and glorious name [to prepare the way for the acknowledgment of Your name by all nations]." –Isaiah 63:14 (Amp)

"One thing I ask of the Lord. This is what I seek—that I may dwell in the house of the Lord all the days of my life, to gaze upon the beauty of the Lord." –Psalm 27:4

My Personal Experience:
_____

_____

You are the BETTER THAN God

"Because Your loving kindness is better than life." –Psalm 63:3
"Better is one day in Your courts than thousands elsewhere." –Psalm 84:10

My Personal Experience:
_____

_____

You are the BLESSED God.

"…Stand up and praise the LORD your God, Who is from everlasting to everlasting. Blessed be Your glorious name, and may it be exalted above all blessing and praise." –Nehemiah 9:5

"And blessed, praised, and glorified be God Most High, Who has given your foes into your hand!" –Genesis 14:20 (Amp)

My Personal Experience:
_____

_____

You are the God Who BLESSES me.

"But there will be no poor among you, for the Lord will surely bless you in the land which the Lord your God gives you for an inheritance to possess", –Deuteronomy 15:4 (Amp)

"The Lord blesses His people with peace." –Psalm 29:11

"The same Lord is Lord of all and richly blesses all who call on Him." –Romans 10:12

My Personal Experience:
_____

_____

You are the BUILDER God.

"Unless the LORD builds the house, its builders labor in vain. Unless the LORD watches over the city, the watchmen stand guard in vain." –Psalm 127:1

"For every house is built by someone, but God is the builder of everything." –Hebrews 3:4

"For he was looking forward to the city with foundations, whose architect and builder is God." –Hebrews 11:10

My Personal Experience:

You are the God who is BOUNTIFUL.

"Your people settle in and from your bounty O God you provide for them." –Psalm 68:10

"What shall I render to the Lord for all His benefits toward me? [How can I repay Him for all His bountiful dealings?" –Psalm 116:12 (Amp)

For I am well assured and indeed know that through your prayers and a bountiful supply of the Spirit of Jesus Christ (the Messiah) this will turn out for my preservation." –Philippians 1:19 (Amp)

My Personal Experience:

You are the God who BEARS MY BURDENS

"Praise be to the Lord, to God our Savior, who daily bears our burdens." –Psalm 68:19

"Cast your burden on the Lord and He will sustain you..." –Psalm 55:22 (NKJV)

My Personal Experience:

You are the God who BINDS up the broken hearted

"He heals the broken hearted and binds up their wounds." –Psalm 147:3

"...The Lord binds up the bruises of his people and heals the wounds He inflicted." –Isaiah 3:26

My Personal Experience:

You are the BELOVED God.

"Here is my servant whom I have chosen, the One I love, in whom I delight..." –Matthew 12:18

"To the praise of His glorious grace, which He has freely given us in the One He loves." –Ephesians 1:6

My Personal Experience:

You are the God who was there in the BEGINNING.

"I [Wisdom] was inaugurated and ordained from everlasting, from the beginning, before ever the earth existed." –Proverbs 8:23 (Amp)

"Who has prepared and done this, calling forth and guiding the destinies of the generations [of the nations] from the beginning? I, the Lord––the first [existing before history began] and with the last [an ever-present, unchanging God]–I am He." –Isaiah 41:4 (Amp)

"I am the Alpha and the Omega, the First and the Last, the Beginning and the End." –Revelation 22:13

"In the beginning, God created the heavens and the earth." –Genesis 1:1

My Personal Experience:

You are the BRIDEGROOM God.

"He who has the bride is the bridegroom;" –John 3:29 (Amp)

"As a young man marries a maiden, so will your sons marry you; as a bridegroom rejoices over his bride, so will your God rejoice over you." –Isaiah 62:5

"Let us rejoice and be glad and give Him glory! For the wedding of the Lamb has come, and His bride has made herself ready." –Revelation 19:7

"For your Maker is your husband– the LORD Almighty is His name– the Holy One of Israel is your Redeemer; He is called the God of all the earth." –Isaiah 54:5

"Go forth daughters of Zion and see King Solomon (–Jesus) with the crown with which His mother crowned Him on the day of His wedding." –Song of Songs 3:11

My Personal Experience:

You are the BRIGHT STAR and cause us to shine like the stars in heaven

"I, Jesus, have sent my angel to give you this testimony for the churches. I am the Root and the Offspring of David, and the bright Morning Star."–Revelation 22:16

"Who is this that appears like the dawn, fair as the moon, bright as the sun, majestic as the stars in procession?" –Song of Solomon 6:10

"Those who are wise will shine like the brightness of the heavens, and those who lead many to righteousness, like the stars forever and ever." –Daniel 12:3

"So that you may become blameless and pure, children of God without fault in a crooked and depraved generation, in which you shine like stars in the universe." –Philippians 2:15

My Personal Experience:

You are the BRANCH of righteousness.

"In that day the Branch of the LORD will be beautiful and glorious, and the fruit of the land will be the pride and glory of the survivors in Israel." –Isaiah 4:2

"A shoot will come up from the stump of Jesse; from his roots a Branch will bear fruit." –Isaiah 11:1

"The days are coming," declares the LORD, "when I will raise up to David a righteous Branch, a King who will reign wisely and do what is just and right in the land." –Jeremiah 23:5

"In those days and at that time I will make a righteous Branch sprout from David's line; he will do what is just and right in the land. –Jeremiah 33:15

My Personal Experience:

You are the BREAD of life.

"For the bread of God is He who comes down from heaven and gives life to the world." –John 6:33

"I am the living bread that came down from heaven. If anyone eats of this bread, he will live forever. This bread is my flesh, which I will give for the life of the world." –John 6:51

"Then Jesus declared, "I am the bread of life. He who comes to me will never go hungry, and he who believes in me will never be thirsty… ; I am the bread of life." –John 6:35; 48

My Personal Experience:

You are the God who BREAKS DOWN and removes obstacles in our life.

"For He breaks down gates of bronze and cuts through bars of iron." –Psalm 107:16

"And it will be said: "Build up, build up, prepare the road! Remove the obstacles out of the way of my people." –Isaiah 57:14

"Pass through, pass through the gates! Prepare the way for the people. Build up, build up the highway! Remove the stones. Raise a banner for the nations." –Isaiah 62:10

"He says, 'I removed the burden from their shoulders; their hands were set free from the basket'." –Psalm 81:6

My Personal Experience:

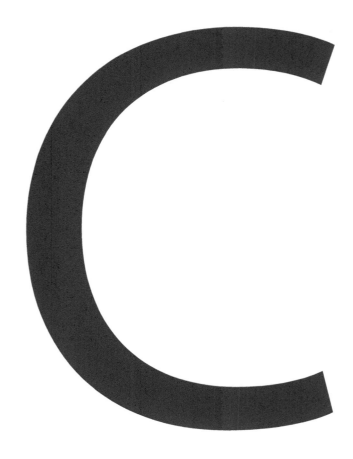

You are the CHRIST.

"Simon Peter answered, 'You are the Christ, the Son of the living God'." –Matthew 16:16

"Today in the town of David a Savior has been born to you; he is Christ the Lord." –Luke 2:11

My Personal Experience:

You are the never CHANGING God.

"For God's gifts and His call are irrevocable. [He never withdraws them when once they are given, and He does not change His mind about those to whom He gives His grace or to whom He sends His call.]" –Romans 11:29 (Amp)

My Personal Experience:

You are the COVENANT keeping God.

"Whenever the rainbow appears in the clouds, I will see it and remember the everlasting covenant between God and all living creatures of every kind on the earth." –Genesis 9:16

"I will establish My covenant as an everlasting covenant between Me and you and your descendants after you for the generations to come, to be your God and the God of your descendants after you." –Genesis 17:7

My Personal Experience:

You are the COUNSELOR God.

"But [only] with [God] are [perfect] wisdom and might; He [alone] has [true] counsel and understanding." –Job 12:13 (Amp)

"I will bless the Lord, Who has given me counsel; yes, my heart instructs me in the night seasons." –Psalm 16:7 (Amp)

My Personal Experience:

You are the CARING God.

"Casting the whole of your care [all your anxieties, all your worries, all your concerns, once and for all] on Him, for He cares for you affectionately and cares about you watchfully. " –1 Peter 5:7 (Amp)

"For He is our God and we are the people of His pasture, the flock under His care." –Psalm 95:7

"You understand, O LORD; remember me and care for me…" –Jeremiah 15:15

My Personal Experience:

You are the CONTENDING God.

"Awake, and rise to my defense! Contend for me, my God and Lord." –Psalm 35:23

"But this is what the LORD says: "Yes, captives will be taken from warriors, and plunder retrieved from the fierce; I will contend with those who contend with you, and your children I will save." –Isaiah 49:25

My Personal Experience:

You are the CHRIST.

"Simon Peter answered, 'You are the Christ, the Son of the living God'." –Matthew 16:16

"Today in the town of David a Savior has been born to you; he is Christ the Lord." –Luke 2:11

My Personal Experience:

You alone are my CONFIDENCE.

"Trust in, lean on, rely on, and have confidence in Him at all times, you people; pour out your hearts before Him. God is a refuge for us (a fortress and a high tower)." –Psalm 62:8 (Amp)

"By fearful and glorious things [that terrify the wicked but make the godly sing praises] do You answer us in righteousness, O God of our salvation, You Who are the confidence and hope of all the ends of the earth and of those far off on the seas," –Psalm 65:5 (Amp)

"For You have been my hope, O Sovereign LORD, my confidence since my youth." –Psalm 71:5

"But blessed is the man who trusts in the LORD, whose confidence is in Him." –Jeremiah 17:7

My Personal Experience:

You are the CHIEF CORNERSTONE.

"Built on the foundation of the apostles and prophets, with Christ Jesus Himself and Chief Cornerstone." –Ephesians 2:20

My Personal Experience: _____

_____

You are our COMFORTER.

"But the Comforter (Counselor, Helper, Intercessor, Advocate, Strengthener, Standby), the Holy Spirit, Whom the Father will send in My name…" –John 14:26 (Amp)

"Who comforts (consoles and encourages) us in every trouble." –2 Corinthians 1:4 (Amp)

"I even I am He that comforts you." –Isaiah 51:12

"But God, Who comforts and encourages and refreshes and cheers the depressed and the sinking…"
–2 Corinthians 7:6 (Amp)

My Personal Experience: _____

_____

You are the CONSOLING God.

"Who comforts (consoles and encourages) us in every trouble (calamity and affliction), so that we may also be able to comfort (console and encourage) those who are in any kind of trouble or distress…" –2 Corinthians 1:4 (Amp)

"When I said "My foot is slipping, Your love O Lord supported me; when anxiety was great within me, Your consolation brought joy to my soul." –Psalm 94:18

My Personal Experience: _____

_____

You are the CLOSE God.

"…The kingdom of God has come close to you." –Luke 10:9 (Amp)

"After she had said this, she went back and called her sister Mary, privately whispering to her, the Teacher is close at hand and is asking for you." –John 11:28 (Amp)

"Come close to God and He will come close to you." – James 4:8 (Amp)

My Personal Experience: _____

_____

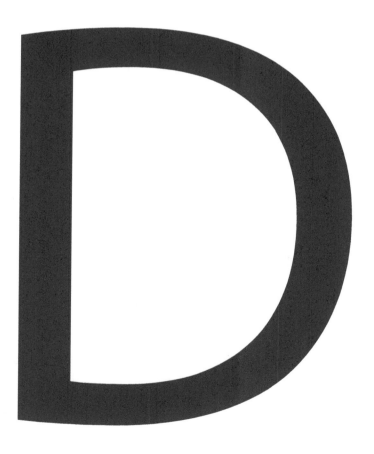

You are the God of all DOMINION.

"How great are His signs! And how mighty His wonders! His kingdom is an everlasting kingdom, and His dominion is from generation to generation." –Daniel 4:3 (Amp)

"He [Christ] shall have dominion also from sea to sea and from the River [Euphrates] to the ends of the earth." –Psalm 72:8 (Amp)

"Your kingdom is an everlasting kingdom, and Your dominion endures throughout all generations." –Psalm 145:13 (Amp)

"For dominion belongs to the Lord and He rules over nations." –Psalm 22:28

My Personal Experience:

You are the DELIVERER God.

"He said: 'The Lord is my Rock and my Fortress and my Deliverer;'" –2 Samuel 22:2 (Amp)

"And so all Israel will be saved, as it is written: 'The deliverer will come from Zion; he will turn godlessness away from Jacob'." – Romans 11:26

"From the Lord comes deliverance." –Psalm 3:8

"Blessed is He who has regard for the weak the Lord delivers him in times of trouble, the Lord will protect him and preserve his life." –Psalm 41:1

My Personal Experience:

You are the DEFENDER God.

"My defense and shield depend on God, Who saves the upright in heart." –Psalm 7:10 (Amp)

"Unto You, O my Strength, I will sing praises; for God is my Defense, my Fortress, and High Tower, the God Who shows me mercy and steadfast love." –Psalm 59:17 (Amp)

"You are the defender of the fatherless and the oppressed…" –Psalm 10:18

"A father to the fatherless, a defender of the widow is God in His dwelling place." –Psalm 68:5

My Personal Experience:

You are the DESIRE of the Nations

"'And I will shake all nations and they shall come to the Desire of all nations, and I will fill this temple with glory', says the Lord of Hosts." –Haggai 2:7

"Whom have I in heaven but You? And I have no delight or desire on earth besides You." –Psalm 73:25 (Amp)

"Yes, LORD, walking in the way of Your laws, we wait for You; Your name and renown are the desire of our hearts." –Isaiah 26:8

"And I will shake the nations and they will come to the Desire of all the Nations and I will fill this temple with glory." –Haggai 2:7

My Personal Experience:

You are the DELIGHTFUL God who delights in me.

"He brought me out into a spacious place; He rescued me because He delighted in me." –2 Samuel 22:20

"Commit yourself to the LORD; let Him deliver him; Let Him rescue him, because He delights in him."–Psalm 22:8
"As for the saints who are in the land, they are the glorious ones in whom is all my delight." –Psalm 16:3

"They feast on the abundance of your house; you give them drink from your river of delights." –Psalm 36:8

"For the LORD takes delight in his people; he crowns the humble with salvation." –Psalm 149:4

"Then I (Wisdom) was the craftsman at His side. I was filled with delight day after day, rejoicing always in His presence, rejoicing in His whole world and delighting in mankind." –Proverbs 8:30–31

My Personal Experience:

You are the DOOR.

"So Jesus said to them again, "Truly, truly, I say to you, I am the door of the sheep. " –John 10:7

"I am the door; if anyone enters through Me, he will be saved, and will go in and out and find pasture." –John 10:9

"The man who enters by the gate is the shepherd of his sheep; I am the gate; whoever enters through me will be saved. He will come in and go out, and find pasture." –John 10:2; 9

My Personal Experience:

You are the DAY STAR.

"And we have the word of the prophets made more certain, and you will do well to pay attention to it, as to a light shining in a dark place, until the day dawns and the Morning Star rises in your hearts." –2 Peter 1:19

My Personal Experience:

You are the EVERLASTING FATHER.

"David praised the LORD in the presence of the whole assembly, saying, "Praise be to you, O LORD, God of our father Israel, from everlasting to everlasting." –1 Chronicles 29:10

For to us a child is born, to us a son is given, and the government will be on his shoulders. And He will be called Wonderful Counselor, Mighty God, Everlasting Father, Prince of Peace." –Isaiah 9:6

My Personal Experience:

You are the ENCOURAGING God.

"And Who has extended His mercy and steadfast love to me before the king, his counselors, and all the king's mighty officers. I was strengthened and encouraged, for the hand of the Lord my God was upon me," –Ezra 7:28 (Amp)

"For whatever was thus written in former days was written for our instruction, that by [our steadfast and patient] endurance and the encouragement [drawn] from the Scriptures we might hold fast to and cherish hope." –Romans 15:4 (Amp)

"You hear O Lord the desire of the afflicted. You encourage them and listen to their cry." –Psalm 10:17

My Personal Experience:

You are the EVERLASTING God.

"Your righteous testimonies are everlasting and Your decrees are binding to eternity; " –Psalm 119:144 (Amp)

"So trust in the Lord (commit yourself to Him, lean on Him, hope confidently in Him) forever; for the Lord God is an everlasting Rock [the Rock of Ages]." –Isaiah 26:4 (Amp)

"Your sun shall no more go down, nor shall your moon withdraw itself, for the Lord shall be your everlasting light, and the days of your mourning shall be ended. "–Isaiah 60:20 (Amp)

"Even from everlasting to everlasting, you are God." –Psalm 90:2

My Personal Experience:

You are ENTHRONED on our praise.

"Sing praises to the LORD, enthroned in Zion; proclaim among the nations what he has done." –Psalm 9:11

"The LORD sits enthroned over the flood; the LORD is enthroned as King forever." –Psalm 29:10

"But you are Holy, enthroned on the praises of Israel." –Psalm 22:3

My Personal Experience:

You are the EVER LOVING God.

"The LORD appeared to us in the past, saying: "I have loved you with an everlasting love; I have drawn you with loving–kindness." –Jeremiah 31:3

"But from everlasting to everlasting the LORD's love is with those who fear him, and his righteousness with their children's children" –Psalm 103:17

"For God so loved the world that He gave His only begotten son, that we who ever believes in Him should not perish but have eternal life." –John 3:16

My Personal Experience: _____

_____

You are the ENDURING God.

"Give thanks to the LORD, for He is good; His love endures forever." –1 Chronicles 16:34

"He will endure as long as the sun, as long as the moon, through all generations." –Psalm 72:5

"But you, O LORD, sit enthroned forever; Your renown endures through all generations." –Psalm 102:12

"May the God who gives endurance and encouragement give you a spirit of unity. –Romans 15:5

My Personal Experience: _____

_____

You are EMMANUEL.

"The virgin will be with child and will give birth to a son, and they will call Him Emmanuel–which means, "God with us." –Matthew 1:23

My Personal Experience: _____

_____

You are the EVER-PRESENT God.

"God is our refuge and strength, an ever present help in trouble." –Psalm 46:1

My Personal Experience: _____

_____

You are the FORGIVING God

"Who forgives all your iniquities, Who heals all your diseases," –Psalm 103:3 (Amp)

"Who is a God like You, Who forgives iniquity and passes over the transgression of the remnant of His heritage? He retains not His anger forever, because He delights in mercy and loving–kindness." –Micah 7:18 (Amp)

"I will confess my transgressions to the Lord, and You forgave the guilt of my sin." –Psalm 32:5

"You are forgiving and good, O Lord; abounding in love to all who call to you." –Psalm 68:5

"The Lord our God is merciful and forgiving." –Daniel 9:9

My Personal Experience:

You are FAITHFUL & true.

"I saw heaven standing open and there before me was a white horse, whose rider is called Faithful and True. With justice He judges and makes war." –Revelation 19:11

"For the word of the Lord is right and true; He is faithful in all He does." –Psalm 33:4

He who calls you is faithful, who also will do it." –1 Thessalonians 5:24

The faithfulness of the Lord endures forever and ever." –Psalm 117:2

My Personal Experience:

You are the FULFILLING God, who fulfills Your purposes in my life.

"And the Lord has fulfilled His promise which He made: You are a father to the widow and the orphan." –1 Kings 8:20 (Amp)

"And You have fulfilled Your promise, for You are just and righteous." –Nehemiah 9:8 (Amp)

"I cry out to God most high, to God who fulfills His purposes for me." –Psalm 57:2

My Personal Experience:

You are the FOREVER God.

"The LORD reigns forever; He has established His throne for judgment." –Psalm 9:7

"To the only God our Savior be glory, majesty, power and authority, through Jesus Christ our Lord, before all ages, now and forevermore! Amen." –Jude 1:25

"For this God is our God for ever and ever. He will be our guide even to the end." –Psalm 48:14

My Personal Experience:

You are the FATHER to the widow and the orphan.

"He defends the cause of the fatherless and the widow, and loves the alien, giving him food and clothing." –Deuteronomy 10:18

"The LORD watches over the alien and sustains the fatherless and the widow, but He frustrates the ways of the wicked." –Psalm 146:9

"A father to the fatherless and a defender of widows is God in His holy dwelling." –Psalm 68:5

My Personal Experience:

You are the God who FEEDS me.

"Taking the five loaves and the two fish and looking up to heaven, He gave thanks and broke the loaves… They all ate and were satisfied, and the disciples picked up twelve basketfuls of broken pieces of bread and fish. The number of the men who had eaten was five thousand." –Mark 6:41–44

"Consider the ravens: They do not sow or reap, they have no storeroom or barn; yet God feeds them. And how much more valuable you are than birds!" –Luke 12:24

"This is the bread that came down from heaven. Your forefathers ate manna and died, but he who feeds on this bread will live forever." –John 6:58

"But you would be fed with the finest of wheat; with honey from the rock I would satisfy you." –Psalm 81:16

My Personal Experience:

You are the God who is FOR me.

"Then my enemies will turn back when I call for help. By this I will know that God is for me." –Psalm 56:9

"What can be said in response to this; "If our God is for us, who can be against us?" –Romans 8:31

My Personal Experience:

You are the God who is the FOUNTAIN of life.

"For with you is the fountain of life; in your light we see light." –Psalm 36:9

"And He said to me, It is done! I am the Alpha and the Omega, the Beginning and the End. To the thirsty I will give water without price from the fountain of the water of Life." –Revelation 21:6 (Amp)

My Personal Experience:

You are the FRIEND to all.

"No one has greater love than to lay down his own life for his friends." –John 15:13 (Amp)

"And the Scripture was fulfilled that says, 'Abraham believed in God, and this was accounted to him as righteousness', and he was called God's friend." –James 2:23 (Amp)

"You are a friend of sinners." –Matthew 11:19

My Personal Experience:

You are the FORERUNNER who goes before us.

"Where Jesus has entered as a forerunner for us, having become a high priest forever according to the order of Melchizedek. –Hebrews 6:20 (NASB)

"But you will not leave in haste or go in flight; for the LORD will go before you, the God of Israel will be your rear guard." –Isaiah 52:12

"I will go before you and will level the mountains; I will break down gates of bronze and cut through bars of iron." –Isaiah 45:2

"Now go, lead the people to the place I spoke of, and My angel will go before you..." –Exodus 32:34

My Personal Experience:

You alone are GOD.

"Now, O LORD our God, deliver us from his hand, so that all kingdoms on earth may know that You alone,

O LORD, are God." –2 Kings 19:19

"For You are great and do marvelous deeds; You alone are God." Psalm 86:10

"O LORD Almighty, God of Israel, enthroned between the cherubim, You alone are God over all the kingdoms of
the earth. You have made heaven and earth." –Isaiah 37:16

"Do you not know, have you not heard? The Lord is the everlasting God, the creator of the ends of the earth." –Isaiah 40:28

My Personal Experience:

You are the God who GUIDES me.

"God is my strong Fortress; He guides the blameless in His way and sets him free." –2 Samuel 22:33 (Amp)

"...He guides me in paths of righteousness..." –Psalm 23:3

"He guides the humble in what is right." –Psalm 25:9

"Guide me with your truth." –Psalm 25:5

My Personal Experience:

You are the GOOD SHEPHERD.

"For the Lamb at the center of the throne will be their shepherd; He will lead them to springs of living water. And God will wipe
away every tear from their eyes." –Revelation 7:17

"The LORD is my shepherd; I shall not be in want." –Psalm 23:1

"I have other sheep that are not of this sheep pen. I must bring them also. They too will listen to my voice, and there shall be
one flock and one shepherd." –John 10:16

"I am the good shepherd. The good shepherd lays down his life for the sheep… I am the good shepherd; I know my sheep
and my sheep know me." –John 10:11; 14

My Personal Experience:

You are the God who GUARDS and protects my life.

"For He will command His angels concerning you to guard you in all your ways;" –Psalm 91:11

"For He guards the course of the just and protects the way of His faithful ones." –Proverbs 2:8

"Guard my life and rescue me, let me not be put to shame for I take refuge in You." –Psalm 31:19

My Personal Experience:

You alone are the GREAT God.

"Do not be terrified by them, for the LORD your God, Who is among you, is a great and awesome God." –Deuteronomy 7:21 (Amp)

"Therefore You are great, O Lord God; for none is like You," –2 Samuel 7:22 (Amp)

"And Ezra blessed the Lord, the great God." –Nehemiah 8:6 (Amp)

"Great is the Lord, and highly to be praised in the city of our God! His holy mountain," –Psalm 48:1 (Amp)

"For great is your love toward me. You have delivered me from the depths of the grave." –Psalm 81:13

My Personal Experience:

You are the GRACIOUS God.

"Yet in Your great mercies You did not utterly consume them or forsake them, for You are a gracious and merciful God." –Nehemiah 9:31 (Amp)

"He will surely be gracious to you at the sound of your cry; when He hears it, He will answer you." –Isaiah 30:19 (Amp)

"You O Lord, are a compassionate and gracious God, slow to anger, abounding in Love and Faithfulness." –Psalm 86:15

My Personal Experience:

You are the GLAD God who makes us glad by all you do.

"For You make him to be blessed and a blessing forever; You make him exceedingly glad with the joy of Your presence." –Psalm 21:6 (Amp)

"Let all those that seek and require You rejoice and be glad in You; let such as love Your salvation say continually, 'The Lord be magnified!'" –Psalm 40:16 (Amp)

"For you make me glad by your deeds, O Lord." –Psalm 92:4

My Personal Experience:

You are the God who is GOOD.

"For the Lord is good and His love endures forever; His faithfulness continues through all generations." –Psalm 100:5

"Taste and see that the Lord is good." –Psalm 34:8

My Personal Experience:

You are the GIVER of good gifts.

"For out of His fullness we have all received one grace after another and spiritual blessing upon spiritual blessing and even favor upon favor and gift upon gift." –John 1:16 (Amp)

"If you, then, though you are evil, know how to give good gifts to your children, how much more will your Father in heaven give good gifts to those who ask Him!" –Matthew 7:11

"I will give you the treasures of darkness, riches stored in secret places so that you may know that I am the Lord, the God of Israel who summons you by name." –Isaiah 45:3

"May the God of our Lord Jesus Christ, the Father of Glory, give you a spirit of wisdom and revelation in the knowledge of Him." –Ephesians 1:17

"For the Lord gives skillful and godly Wisdom; from His mouth come knowledge and understanding." –Proverbs 2:6 (Amp)

"He changes the times and the seasons; He removes kings and sets up kings. He gives wisdom to the wise and knowledge to those who have understanding!" –Daniel 2:21 (Amp)

"To the man who pleases Him, God gives wisdom, knowledge and happiness." –Ecclesiastes 2:26

My Personal Experience: _____

_____

You are the God who is GUARDIAN of my soul.

"For You were continually straying like sheep, but now you have returned to the Shepherd and guardian of your souls."
–1 Peter 2:25 (NASB)

My Personal Experience: _____

_____

You are the GLORIOUS God.

"He Himself became as much superior to angels as the glorious Name which He has inherited is different from and more excellent than theirs." –Hebrews 1:4 (Amp)

"On the glorious splendor of Your majesty and on Your wondrous works I will meditate." –Psalm 145:5

"I keep asking that the God of our Lord Jesus Christ, the glorious Father, may give you the Spirit of wisdom and revelation, so that you may know him better." –Ephesians 1:17

"In that day the branch of the Lord will be beautiful and glorious." –Isaiah 4:12

"Praise Your glorious name." –I Chronicles 24:13

My Personal Experience: _____

_____

You are the GIFT to me.

"For since He Whom God has sent speaks the words of God, God does not give Him His Spirit sparingly or by measure, but boundless is the gift God makes of His Spirit!" –John 3:34 (Amp)

"Peter replied, 'Repent and be baptized, every one of you, in the name of Jesus Christ for the forgiveness of your sins. And you will receive the gift of the Holy Spirit.'" –Acts 2:38

"Jesus answered her, "If you knew the gift of God and who asks you for a drink..." –John 4:10

My Personal Experience:
_____

_____

You are the GIVER of wisdom.

"To the man who pleases Him, God gives wisdom, knowledge and happiness..."-Ecclesiastes 2:26

My Personal Experience:
_____

_____

You are the God of HOPE.

"For in You, O Lord, do I hope; You will answer, O Lord my God." –Psalm 38:15 (Amp)

"The Lord is my portion or share, says my living being; therefore will I hope in Him and wait expectantly for Him." –Lamentations 3:24 (Amp)

"You answer us with awesome deeds of righteousness, O God our Savior, the hope of all the ends of the earth and of the farthest seas," –Psalm 65:5

"And hope does not put us to shame, because God's love has been poured out into our hearts through the Holy Spirit, who has been given to us." –Romans 5:5

"To them God has chosen to make known among the Gentiles the glorious riches of this mystery, which is Christ in you, the hope of glory." –Colossians 1:27

My Personal Experience:

You are the HEIR of all things.

"Ask of me, and I will make the nations your inheritance, the ends of the earth your possession." –Psalm 2:8

My Personal Experience:

You are the God who HEARS me.

"With my voice I cry to the Lord, and He hears and answers me out of His holy hill." –Psalm 3:4 (Amp)

"The Lord listens and heeds when I call to Him." –Psalm 4:3 (Amp)

My Personal Experience:

You are the God who is my HELPER.

"Hear, O Lord, have mercy and be gracious to me! O Lord, be my helper!" –Psalm 30:10 (Amp)

"Behold, God is my helper and ally; the Lord is my upholder and is with them who uphold my life." –Psalm 54:4 (Amp)

"So we take comfort and are encouraged and confidently and boldly say, The Lord is my Helper…" –Hebrews 13:6 (Amp)

My Personal Experience:

You are my HIDING PLACE.

"..You hide me in the shadow of your wings." - Psalm 10:14

""We wait in hope for the Lord; He is our help and our shield." - Psalm 33:20

"...You are my help and my deliverer, O my God, do not delay." -Psalm 40:17

My Personal Experience:

You are the HEALER God.

"… I am the Lord Who heals you." –Exodus 15:26 (Amp)

"Who heals [each one of] all your diseases," –Psalm 103:3 (Amp)

"He heals the brokenhearted and binds up their wounds." –Psalm 147:3 (Amp)

"But He was pierced for our transgressions, crushed for our iniquities." –Isaiah 53:5

My Personal Experience:

You are the HAPPY God.

"The LORD your God is with you, He is mighty to save. He will take great delight in you, He will quiet you with His love, He will rejoice over you with singing." –Zephaniah 3:17 (Amp)

"Therefore your God has anointed you with oil of gladness more than your companions." –Hebrews 1:9

My Personal Experience:

You are the HOLY ONE.

"For I am the Lord your God; so consecrate yourselves and be holy, for I am holy;" –Leviticus 11:44 (Amp)

"There is none holy like the Lord, there is none besides You; there is no Rock like our God." –1 Samuel 2:2 (Amp)

"Glory in His holy name; let the hearts of those rejoice who seek the Lord!" –1 Chronicles 16:10 (Amp)

"This is what the LORD says—the Redeemer and Holy One of Israel—to him who was despised and abhorred by the nation, to the servant of rulers: 'Kings will see you and rise up, princes will see and bow down, because of the LORD, who is faithful, the Holy One of Israel, who has chosen you'." –Isaiah 49:7

"Holy, holy, holy is the Lord God almighty, the whole earth is full of His glory." –Isaiah 6:3

My Personal Experience:

You are the God who INSTRUCTS me.

"Know also in your hearts that, as a man disciplines and instructs his son, so the Lord your God disciplines and instructs you." –Deuteronomy 8:5 (Amp)

"…For his God instructs him correctly and teaches him." –Isaiah 28:26 (Amp)

"I will instruct you and teach you in the way you should go." –Psalm 32:8

My Personal Experience:

You are the God of INCREASE.

"Hear therefore, O Israel, and be watchful to do them, that it may be well with you and that you may increase exceedingly, as the Lord, the God of your fathers, has promised you, in a land flowing with milk and honey." –Deuteronomy 6:3 (Amp)

"There [the Lord] greatly increased His people and made them stronger than their oppressors." –Psalm 105:24 (Amp)

"You have increased the nation, O Lord; You have increased the nation." –Isaiah 26:15 (Amp)

"May the Lord make your love to increase." –Ephesians 2:7

"Of the increase of His government and peace there will be no end." –Isaiah 9:7

"The apostles said the Lord "Increase our faith." –Luke 17:5

My Personal Experience:

You are the God of the IMPOSSIBLE.

"For nothing is impossible with God." –Luke 1:37

"He divided the sea and led them through; He made the water stand firm like a wall." –Psalm 78:13

My Personal Experience:

Your are the INCOMPARABLE God.

"Behold, even the moon has no brightness [compared to God's glory] and the stars are not pure in His sight." –Job 25:5 (Amp)

"For who in the heavens can be compared to the Lord? Who among the mighty [heavenly beings] can be likened to the Lord." –Psalm 89:6

"That He might show the incomparable riches of His grace." –Ephesians 2:7

My Personal Experience:

You are the God of INHERITANCE.

"By having the eyes of your heart flooded with light, so that you can know and understand the hope to which He has called you, and how rich is His glorious inheritance in the saints (His set–apart ones)," –Ephesians 1:18 (Amp)

"For the LORD's portion is His people, Jacob His allotted inheritance." –Deuteronomy 32:9

"The Lord is their inheritance…" –Deuteronomy 10:9

"The people He chose for His inheritance." –Psalm 33:12

My Personal Experience:

You are the INTERCESSOR.

"And He Who searches the hearts of men knows what is in the mind of the [Holy] Spirit, because the Spirit intercedes and pleads in behalf of the saints according to and in harmony with God's will." –Romans 8:27 (Amp)

"He always lives to intercede for them." –Hebrews 7:25

"Christ Jesus, who died, more than that raised from the dead, is at the right hand of God, and is also interceding for us." –Romans 8:34

My Personal Experience:

You are the IMMORTAL and INVISIBLE God.

"Which God will bring about in His own time–God, the blessed and only Ruler, the King of kings and Lord of lords, Who alone is immortal and Who lives in unapproachable light, whom no one has seen or can see. To Him be honor and might forever. Amen." –1 Timothy 6:15–16

"He is the image of the invisible God, the firstborn over all creation." –Colossians 1:15

"Now to the King eternal immortal invincible, the only God" –1 Timothy 1:17

My Personal Experience:

You are the INVINCIBLE God.

"The Lord God is my strength, my personal bravery, and my invincible army;" –Habakkuk 3:19 (Amp)

"Now to the King eternal immortal invincible, the only God" –1 Timothy 1:17

My Personal Experience:

You are the God who is INVITING.

"For the promise is to and for you and your children, and to and for all that are far away, to and for as many as the Lord our God invites and bids to come to Himself." –Acts 2:39 (Amp)

"My lover spoke and said to me, "Arise, my darling, my beautiful one, and come away with me." –Song of Solomon 2:10

"Go therefore to the main highways, and as many as you find there, invite to the wedding feast." –Matthew 22:9

"He has consecrated those He has invited." –Zephaniah 1:7

My Personal Experience:

You are the INDESCRIBABLE God.

"Now thanks be to God for His Gift, [precious] beyond telling [His indescribable, inexpressible, free Gift]!" –2 Corinthians 9:15 (Amp)

"Who is like You, O Lord, among the gods? Who is like You, glorious in holiness, awesome in splendor, doing wonders?" –Exodus 15:11 (Amp)

"Thanks be to God for His indescribable gift." –2 Corinthians 9:15

My Personal Experience:

You are JESUS CHRIST

"...Jesus Christ the son of David, the son of Abraham."-Matthew 1:1

"My dear children, I write this to you so that you will not sin. But if anybody does sin, we have one who speaks to the Father in our defense- Jesus Christ, the Righteous One." -1 John 2:1

My Personal Experience:

You are the God who is the righteous JUDGE.

"Shall not the Judge of all the earth execute judgment and do righteously?" –Genesis 18:25 (Amp)

"I have fought the good fight, I have finished the race, I have kept the faith. Finally, there is laid up for me the crown of righteousness, which the Lord, the righteous Judge, will give to me on that Day, and not to me only but also to all who have loved His appearing." –2 Timothy 4:7–8(Amp)

"God is a righteous judge." –Psalm 7:1

My Personal Experience:

You are the JEALOUS God.

"For you shall worship no other god; for the Lord, Whose name is Jealous, is a jealous God," –Exodus 34:14 (Amp)

"The Lord your God is a jealous God." –Exodus 20:5

"God is a consuming fire, a jealous God." –Deuteronomy 4:24

My Personal Experience:

You are the God of JOY.

"He will yet fill your mouth with laughter and your lips with shouts of joy." –Job 8:21

"You have made known to me the path of life; you will fill me with joy in your presence, with eternal pleasures at your right hand." –Psalm 16:11

"Then will I go to the altar of God, to God, my joy and my delight. I will praise you with the harp, O God, my God." –Psalm 43:4

"You love righteousness and hate wickedness; therefore God, your God, has set you above your companions by anointing you with the oil of joy." –Psalm 45:7

"These I will bring to my holy mountain and give them joy in my house of prayer..." –Isaiah 56:7

"…Do not grieve, for the joy of the LORD is your strength." –Nehemiah 8:10

My Personal Experience:

You are the KING forever.

"The Lord sat as King over the deluge; the Lord sits as King forever!" –Psalm 29:10 (Amp)

"Now to the King of eternity, incorruptible and immortal, invisible, the only God, be honor and glory forever and ever. Amen" –1 Timothy 1:17 (Amp)

"You are King forever and ever." –Psalm 10:16

My Personal Experience:

You are the God who is the KING OF ISRAEL.

"Thus says the Lord, the King of Israel and his Redeemer, the Lord of hosts: 'I am the first and I am the last, and there is no God besides Me.'" –Isaiah 44:6 (Amp)

"The Lord has taken away your punishment; He has turned back your enemy. The Lord, the King of Israel, is with you; never again will you fear any harm." –Zephaniah 3:15

"They took palm branches and went out to meet him, shouting, 'Hosanna! Blessed is he who comes in the name of the Lord! Blessed is the King of Israel!'" –John 12:13

"He saved others," they said, "but He can't save himself! He's the King of Israel! Let him come down now from the cross, and we will believe in Him." –Matthew 27:42

"Then Nathanael declared, 'Rabbi, you are the Son of God; you are the King of Israel'." –John 1:49

My Personal Experience:

You are the KIND God.

"He gives his king great victories; he shows unfailing kindness to his anointed, to David and his descendants forever." –Psalm 18:50

"But let him who boasts boast about this: that he understands and knows me, that I am the LORD, who exercises kindness, justice and righteousness on earth, for in these I delight', declares the LORD." –Jeremiah 9:24

"The LORD appeared to us in the past, saying: 'I have loved you with an everlasting love; I have drawn you with loving–kindness.'" –Jeremiah 31:3

My Personal Experience:

You Are the KING OF KINGS and Lord of Lords.

"...Which God will bring about in his own time-God, the blessed and only Ruler, the King of Kings and Lord of lords." -1 Timothy 6:15

My Personal Experience:

You are the LIGHT OF THE WORLD

"When Jesus spoke again to the people, he said, "I am the light of the world. Whoever follows me will never walk in darkness, but will have the light of life." -John 8:12

"While I am in the world, I am the light of the world." -John 9:5

"The Lord is my light and my salvation..."-Psalm 27:1

My Personal Experience:

You are the perfect LEADER.

"He makes me lie down in green pastures; He leads me beside the still and restful waters." –Psalm 23:2 (Amp)

"He refreshes and restores my life; He leads me in the paths of righteousness for His name's sake." –Psalm 23:3 (Amp)

"See, I have made him a witness to the peoples, a leader and commander of the peoples." –Isaiah 55:4

My Personal Experience:

You are the LAUGHING God

"The One enthroned in heaven laughs..." Psalm 2:4

My Personal Experience:

You are the LISTENING God.

"But know that the Lord has set apart for Himself him who is godly. The Lord listens and heeds when I call to Him." –Psalm 4:3 (Amp)

"With my voice I cry to the Lord, and He hears and answers me out of His holy hill." –Psalm 3:4 (Amp)

"You hear O Lord, the desires of the afflicted. You encourage them and listen to their cry." –Psalm 10:17

My Personal Experience:

You are the LOVING God.

"Beloved, let us love one another, for love is (springs) from God;" –1 John 4:7 (Amp)

"The Lord loves the just and will not forsake His faithful ones." –Psalm 37:28

"For as high as the heavens are above the earth, so great is His love for those who fear Him." –Psalm 103:11

"For great is your love toward me, You have delivered me from the depths of the grave." –Psalm 81:13

"For God so loved the world that He gave His only begotten son, that whoever believes in Him shall not perish but have eternal life." –John 3:16

My Personal Experience:

_____

_____

You are the LION of the tribe of Judah.

"The lion has roared– who will not fear? The Sovereign LORD has spoken– who can but prophesy?" –Amos 3

"Then one of the elders said to me, 'Do not weep! See, the Lion of the tribe of Judah, the Root of David, has triumphed. He is able to open the scroll and its seven seals'." –Revelation 5:5

My Personal Experience:

_____

_____

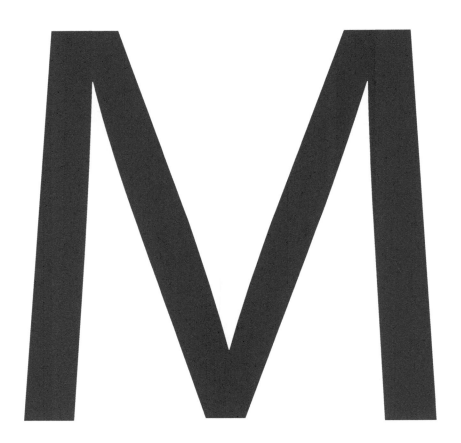

You are the MIGHTY God.

"Behold! God is mighty, and yet despises no one nor regards anything as trivial; He is mighty in power of understanding and heart." –Job 36:5 (Amp)

"O Lord God, You have only begun to show Your servant Your greatness and Your mighty hand…" –Deuteronomy 3:24 (Amp)

"For the Lord your God is God of gods and Lord of lords, the great, the mighty, the terrible God, Who is not partial and takes no bribe." –Deuteronomy 10:17 (Amp)

"Who is this King of Glory, the Lord strong and mighty, the Lord mighty in battle." –Psalm 24:8

My Personal Experience:

You are the MINDFUL God.

"For He performs [that which He has] planned for me, and of many such matters He is mindful." –Job 23:14 (Amp)

"He is mindful of His covenant and forever it is imprinted on His heart, the word which He commanded and established to a thousand generations." –Psalm 105:8 (Amp)

"The Lord has been mindful of us, He will bless us: He will bless the house of Israel, He will bless the house of Aaron [the priesthood]." –Psalm 115:12 (Amp)

"What is man that You are mindful of him, the son of man that You care for him?" –Psalm 8:4

My Personal Experience:

You are the MERCIFUL God.

"When he cries to Me, I will hear, for I am gracious and merciful." –Exodus 22:27 (Amp)

"For the Lord your God is a merciful God; He will not fail you or destroy you or forget the covenant of your fathers, which He swore to them." –Deuteronomy 4:31 (Amp)

"Yet in Your great mercies You did not utterly consume them or forsake them, for You are a gracious and merciful God." –Nehemiah 9:31 (Amp)

"Have mercy on me, O Lord, for I call to you all day long." –Psalm 86:3

"For this reason he had to be made like his brothers in every way, in order that he might become a merciful and faithful high priest in service to God, and that he might make atonement for the sins of the people." –Hebrews 2:17

My Personal Experience:

You are the MANIFESTING God.

"I will accept you as a pleasant odor when I lead you out from the peoples and gather you out of the countries in which you have been scattered, and I will manifest My holiness among you in the sight of the nations." –Ezekiel 20:41 (Amp)

"And I will manifest My honor and glory among the nations…" –Ezekiel 39:21 (Amp)

"This beginning of His signs Jesus did in Cana of Galilee, and manifested His glory, and His disciples believed in Him." –John 2:11 (NASB)

"But thanks to God, who leads us in triumphal procession in Christ and through us spreads everywhere –manifests the fragrance of the knowledge of Him." –2 Corinthians 2:14-16

My Personal Experience: _____

_____

You are the MEDIATOR.

"For there is one God and one mediator between God and men, the man Christ Jesus." –1 Timothy 2:5

"For this reason Christ is the mediator of a new covenant, that those who are called may receive the promised eternal inheritance– now that He has died as a ransom to set them free from the sins committed under the first covenant." –Hebrews 9:15

"But the ministry Jesus has received is as superior to theirs as the covenant of which he is mediator is superior to the old one, and it is founded on better promises." –Hebrews 8:6

My Personal Experience: _____

_____

You are the MESSIAH.

"Jacob was the father of Joseph the husband of Mary, by whom Jesus was born, who is called the Messiah." –Matthew 1:6

"The LORD (God) says to my Lord (the Messiah), Sit at My right hand, until I make Your adversaries Your footstool." –Psalm 110:1 (Amp)

"And say to him, Thus says the Lord of hosts: [You, Joshua] behold (look at, keep in sight, watch) the Man [the Messiah] whose name is the Branch, for He shall grow up in His place and He shall build the [true] temple of the Lord." –Zechariah 6:12 (Amp)

"The first thing Andrew did was to find his brother Simon and tell him, "We have found the Messiah" –that is, the Christ." –John 1:41

My Personal Experience: _____

_____

You are the MAKER of all things.

"Come, let us bow down in worship, let us kneel before the LORD our Maker;" –Psalm 95:6

"May you be blessed by the LORD, the Maker of heaven and earth." –Psalm 115:5

"Rich and poor have this in common: The LORD is the Maker of them all." –Proverbs 22:2

"For your Maker is your husband– the LORD Almighty is His name– the Holy One of Israel is your Redeemer; He is called the God of all the earth." –Isaiah 54:5

"For you created my inmost being; you knit me together in my mother's womb." –Psalms 139:19

My Personal Experience _____

_____

You are the NAME ABOVE ALL NAMES God.

""I will bow down toward Your holy temple and will praise Your name for Your love and Your faithfulness, for You have exalted above all things Your name and Your word." –Psalm 138:2

"Let them praise the name of the Lord, for His name alone is exalted; His splendor is above the earth and the heavens." –Psalm 148:13

"Therefore God exalted Him to the highest place and gave Him the name that is above every name," –Philippians 2:9

My Personal Experience: _____

_____

You are the God for whom NOTHING is impossible.

"For with God nothing is ever impossible and no word from God shall be without power or impossible of fulfillment." –Luke 1:37 (Amp)

"He replied, 'Because you have so little faith. I tell you the truth, if you have faith as small as a mustard seed, you can say to this mountain, 'Move from here to there' and it will move. Nothing will be impossible for you." –Matthew 17:20

"Therefore God exalted Him to the highest place and gave Him the name that is above every name," –Philippians 2:9

"Nothing is too hard for You." –Jeremiah 32:17

My Personal Experience: _____

_____

You are the NURTURING God.

"When He went ashore and saw a great throng of people, He had compassion for them and cured their sick." –Matthew 14:14 (Amp)

"You will not break a bruised reed or snuff out a smoldering wick." –Isaiah 42:3

"Therefore God exalted Him to the highest place and gave Him the name that is above every name." –Philippians 2:9

My Personal Experience: _____

_____

You are the God who is NOBLE God.

And since we have [such] a great and wonderful and noble Priest over the house of God..." –Hebrews 10:21 (Amp)

"Therefore God exalted Him to the highest place and gave Him the name that is above every name." –Philippians 2:9

"Listen, for I shall speak noble things" –Proverbs 8:6

"Your attitude should be the same as that of Christ Jesus: Who, being in very nature God, did not consider equality with God something to be grasped, but made Himself nothing, taking the very nature of a servant, being made in human likeness. And being found in appearance as a man, He humbled Himself and became obedient to death – even death on a cross!"

My Personal Experience: _____

_____

You are the NEVER FAILING God.

"Cast your burden on the Lord and He will sustain you; He will never allow the righteous to be moved." –Psalm 55:22 (Amp)

"Therefore, those who are ill–treated and suffer in accordance with God's will must do right and commit their souls to the One Who created [them] and will never fail [them]." –1 Peter 4:19 (Amp)

"Therefore God exalted Him to the highest place and gave Him the name that is above every name," –Philippians 2:9

"God will not in any way fail His beloved or leave her lacking His support. Because He is never failing we should never fear! We will be taken when He deems that it is time for us to be rejoined with Him." –Hebrews 13:5-6

My Personal Experience:

You are the NEW mercy God. Your mercies are new every morning.

"But I will sing of Your mighty strength and power; yes, I will sing aloud of Your mercy and loving–kindness in the morning; for You have been to me a defense (a fortress and a high tower) and a refuge in the day of my distress." –Psalm 59:16

"O satisfy us with Your mercy and loving–kindness in the morning [now, before we are older], that we may rejoice and be glad all our days." –Psalm 90:14

"Therefore God exalted Him to the highest place and gave Him the name that is above every name," –Philippians 2:9

"His mercies are new every morning." –Lamentations 3:23

My Personal Experience:

You are the OPENER of my eyes.

"The Lord opens the eyes of the blind, the Lord lifts up those who are bowed down, the Lord loves the righteous." –Psalm 146:8 (Amp)

"To open the eyes of the blind, to bring out prisoners from the dungeon, and those who sit in darkness from the prison." –Isaiah 42:7 (Amp)

"To open their eyes that they may turn from darkness to light and from the power of Satan to God, so that they may thus receive forgiveness and release from their sins and a place and portion among those who are consecrated and purified by faith in Me." –Acts 26:18 (Amp)

"Open my eyes that I may see wonderful things in Your Law. I am a stranger in the earth. Do not hide Your commands from me." –Psalm 119:18

My Personal Experience:

You are the OVERCOMER God.

"I have told you these things, so that in Me you may have peace and confidence. In the world you have tribulation and trials and distress and frustration; but be of good cheer! For I have overcome the world." –John 16:33 (Amp)

"Who is He that overcomes the world." –1 John 5:5

"But of God, He overcomes the world." –1 John 3:4

My Personal Experience:

You are the ONLY God.

"And there is no other God besides Me, a rigidly and uncompromisingly just and righteous God and Savior; there is none besides Me." –Isaiah 45:21 (Amp)

"Hear, O Israel: The Lord our God, the Lord is one." –Deuteronomy 6:5

"...To the only wise God be glory forever through Jesus Christ! Amen." –Romans 17:27

My Personal Experience:

You are the God who is the ONLY BEGOTTEN OF THE FATHER.

"The Word became flesh and made His dwelling among us. We have seen His glory, the glory of the One and Only, who came from the Father, full of grace and truth." –John 1:14

"No one has seen God at any time; the only begotten God who is in the bosom of the Father, He has explained Him." –John 1:18 (NASB)

"For God so loved the world, that He gave His only begotten Son, that whoever believes in Him shall not perish, but have eternal life." –John 3:16 (NASB)

"By this the love of God was manifested in us, that God has sent His only begotten Son into the world so that we might live through Him." –1 John 4:9

My Personal Experience: _____

_____

You are the God who gave Yourself as an OFFERING for us.

"Abraham answered, "God himself will provide the lamb for the burnt offering, my son." And the two of them went on together." –Genesis 22:8

"Who gave himself for our sins to rescue us from the present evil age, according to the will of our God and Father," –Galatians 1:4

"For there is one God and one mediator between God and men, the man Christ Jesus, who gave himself as a ransom for all men– the testimony given in its proper time." –1 Timothy 2:5–6

"And live a life of love, just as Christ loved us and gave himself up for us as a fragrant offering and sacrifice to God."–Ephesians 5:2

My Personal Experience: _____

_____

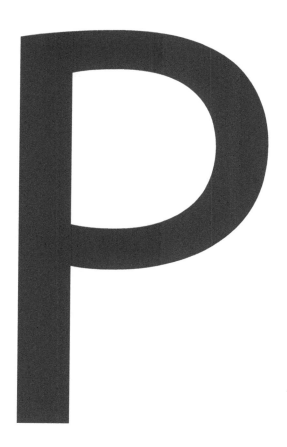

You are the PROTECTING God.

"We know that anyone born of God does not practice committing sin, but the One Who was begotten of God carefully watches over and protects him…" –1 John 5:18

"O my Strength, I will watch and give heed to You and sing praises; for God is my Defense." –Psalm 59:9 (Amp)

"I will protect them from those who making them." –Psalm 12:5

"Because He loves Me," says the Lord, "I will rescue him; I will protect him and honor him, for he acknowledges my name."

My Personal Experience:

You are the PRESENT God.

"…Says the Lord, for I am with you to save you and to deliver you…" –Jeremiah 42:11 (Amp)

"…And surely I am with you always, to the very end of the age." –Matthew 28:20

"For God is present in the company of the righteous." –Psalm 14:5

My Personal Experience:

You are the PRESERVING God.

"In the presence of God, Who preserves alive all living things, and of Christ Jesus…" –1 Timothy 6:13 (Amp)

"O you who love the Lord, hate evil; He preserves the lives of His saints, He delivers them out of the hand of the wicked." –Psalm 97:10 (Amp)

"Love the Lord all you saints, the Lord preserves the faithful." –Psalm 31:23

"I am laid low in the dust; preserve my life according to Your word." –Psalm 119:25

"Your promise preserves my life." –Psalm 119:50

My Personal Experience:

You are the PROMISER OF PEACE.

"Grace, mercy, and peace will be with us, from God the Father and from Jesus Christ, the Father's Son, in all sincerity and love." –2 John 1:3 (Amp)

"Who were chosen and foreknown by God the Father and consecrated by the Spirit to be obedient to Jesus Christ and to be sprinkled with blood: May grace and peace be given you in increasing abundance." –1 Peter 1:2 (Amp)

"He promises peace to His people, the saints." –Psalm 85:8

My Personal Experience:

You are the POWERFUL God.

"And said, O Lord, God of our fathers, are You not God in heaven? And do You not rule over all the kingdoms of the nations? In Your hand are power and might, so that none is able to withstand You." –2 Chronicles 20:6 (Amp)

"Behold! God is mighty, and yet despises no one nor regards anything as trivial; He is mighty in power of understanding and heart." –Job 36:5 (Amp)

"For God did not give us a spirit of timidity, but of power and of love and of calm and well-balanced mind and discipline and self-control." –2 Timothy 1:7 (Amp)

"Your arm is endued with power, your hand is strong. Your right hand is exalted." –Psalm 89:13

My Personal Experience:

You are my PORTION.

"The Lord is my chosen and assigned portion, my cup; You hold and maintain my lot." –Psalm 16:5 (Amp)

"There is need of only one or but a few things. Mary has chosen the good portion which shall not be taken away from her." –Luke 10:42 (Amp)

"This is your lot, the portion measured to you from Me, says the Lord," –Jeremiah 13:25 (Amp)

"You are my portion O Lord." –Psalm 119:57

My Personal Experience:

You are the PERFECTER of my faith.

"May the God of peace, who through the blood of the eternal covenant brought back from the dead our Lord Jesus, that great Shepherd of the sheep, equip you with everything good for doing his will, and may he work in us what is pleasing to him, through Jesus Christ, to whom be glory forever and ever. Amen." –Hebrews 13: 20–21

"Let us fix our eyes on Jesus, the author and perfecter of our faith." –Hebrews 12:2

My Personal Experience:

You are the POTTER God.

"Or does not the potter have a right over the clay, to make from the same lump one vessel for honorable use and another for common use?" –Romans 9:21 (NASB)

"Your hands made me and formed me; give me understanding to learn your commands." –Psalm 119:3

"… He who formed me in the womb to be his servant to bring Jacob back to him and gather Israel to himself… "Because He loves Me," says the Lord, "I will rescue him; I will protect him and honor him, for he acknowledges my name." –Isaiah 49:5

"You are our Father. We are the clay, You are the potter; we are all the work of Your hand." –Isaiah 64:8

My Personal Experience:

You are the God who PURCHASED me.

"But [you were purchased] with the precious blood of Christ like that of a [sacrificial] lamb without blemish or spot." –1 Peter 1:19 (Amp)

"With Your blood You purchased men for God." –Revelations 5:9

My Personal Experience:

You are the PROVIDER God.

"And [God] Who provides seed for the sower and bread for eating will also provide and multiply your sowing and increase the fruits of your righteousness." –2 Corinthians 9:10 (Amp)

"And my God will meet all your needs according to his glorious riches in Christ Jesus." –Philippians 4:19

"He provides food for those who fear Him." –Psalm 111:5

"To put their HOPE in God who richly provides us with everything for our enjoyment." –1 Timothy 6:17

My Personal Experience:

You are the High PRIEST.

"Therefore, holy brothers, who share in the heavenly calling, fix your thoughts on Jesus, the apostle and high priest whom we confess." –Hebrews 3:1

"For we do not have a high priest who is unable to sympathize with our weaknesses, but we have one who has been tempted in every way, just as we are–yet was without sin." –Hebrews 4:15

"He has become a high priest forever." –Psalm 6:20

My Personal Experience:

You are the PRICELESS God.

"Yes, furthermore, I count everything as loss compared to the possession of the priceless privilege of knowing Christ Jesus my Lord." –Philippians 3:8 (Amp)

"How priceless is Your unfailing love." –Psalm 36:7

My Personal Experience:

You are the God of POSSIBILITIES.

"Then God remembered Rachel and answered her pleading and made it possible for her to have children." –Genesis 30:22 (Amp)

My Personal Experience:

You are the God whose PLANS stand forever.

"Many are the plans in a man's heart, but it is the Lord's purpose that prevails." –Proverbs 19:21

"The plans of the Lord stand firm forever." –Psalm 33:11

My Personal Experience:

You are the PRINCE OF PEACE.

"So Gideon built an altar to the Lord there and called it The Lord is Peace…" –Judges 6:24

"The Lord gives strength to His people; the Lord blesses His people with peace." –Psalm 29:11

"You will keep in perfect peace him whose mind is steadfast, because he trusts in You." –Isaiah 26:3

" For to us a child is born, to us a son is given, and the government will be on his shoulders. And He will be called Wonderful Counselor, Mighty God, Everlasting Father, Prince of Peace." –Isaiah 9:6

My Personal Experience:

You are the PROPHET God.

"For the testimony of Jesus is the spirit of prophecy." –Revelation 19:10

"For Moses said, 'The Lord your God will raise up for you a prophet like me from among your own people; you must listen to everything he tells you'." –Acts 3:22

My Personal Experience:

You are the PROPITIATION for our sins

"God presented him as a sacrifice of atonement, through faith in his blood. He did this to demonstrate his justice, because in his forbearance he had left the sins committed beforehand unpunished."-Romans 3:25

"He is the atoning sacrifice for our sins, and not only for ours but also for the sins of the world."-1 John 2:2

My Personal Experience:

You have PITY on the weak.

"He will take pity on the weak and the needy and save the needy from death." -Psalm 72:13

My Personal Experience:

You are the QUICK God.

"And will not [our just] God defend and protect and avenge His elect (His chosen ones), who cry to Him day and night? Will He defer them and delay help on their behalf? I tell you, He will defend and protect and avenge them speedily." –Luke 18:7–8 (Amp)

"And behold, I am coming quickly…" –Revelation 22:7 (Amp)

"Turn your ear to me, come quickly to my rescue, be my rock of salvation, a strong fortress to save all." –Psalm 31:2

My Personal Experience:

You are the God who QUIETS me with Your love.

"The Lord your God in your midst, The Mighty One, will save; He will rejoice over you with gladness, He will quiet you with His love, He will rejoice over you with singing." –Zephaniah 3:17 (Amp)

My Personal Experience:

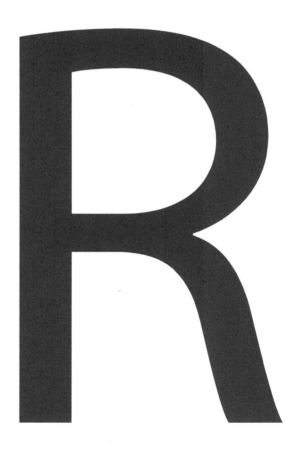

You are my REFUGE.

"The eternal God is your refuge and dwelling place." –Deuteronomy 33:27 (Amp)

"My God, my Rock, in Him will I take refuge; my Shield and the Horn of my salvation; my Stronghold and my Refuge, my Savior–You save me from violence." –2 Samuel 22:3 (Amp)

"Keep and protect me, O God, for in You I have found refuge, and in You do I put my trust and hide myself." –Psalm 16:1 (Amp)

"I will say of the Lord, He is my Refuge and my Fortress, my God; on Him I lean and rely, and in Him I trust!" –Psalm 91:2 (Amp)

"You are a refuge for the oppressed." –Psalm 9:9

My Personal Experience:

You are the REIGNING God.

"Both riches and honor come from You, and You reign over all. In Your hands are power and might; in Your hands it is to make great and to give strength to all." –1 Chronicles 29:12 (Amp)

"For [Christ] must be King and reign until He has put all [His] enemies under His feet." –1 Corinthians 15:25 (Amp)

"The Lord reigns forever." –Psalm 9:7

My Personal Experience:

You are the RULER God.

"This sentence is by the decree of the [heavenly] watchers and the decision is by the word of the holy ones, to the intent that the living may know that the Most High [God] rules the kingdom of mankind." –Daniel 4:17 (Amp)

"And from Jesus Christ the faithful and trustworthy Witness, the Firstborn of the dead and the Prince of the kings of the earth." –Revelation 1:5 (Amp)

"For dominion belongs to the Lord and He rules over nations. –Psalm 22:28

"You rule over the surging sea; when its waves mount up you still them." –Psalm 89:9

My Personal Experience:

You are my ROCK.

"My God, my Rock, in Him will I take refuge; my Shield and the Horn of my salvation; my Stronghold and my refuge, my Savior–You save me from violence." –2 Samuel 22:3 (Amp)

"But the Lord has become my High Tower and Defense, and my God the Rock of my refuge." –Psalm 94:22 (Amp)

"Turn your ear to me, come quickly to my rescue, be my rock of refuge, a strong fortress to save me." –Psalm 31:2

My Personal Experience:

You are my REDEEMER.

"Who redeems your life from the pit and corruption, Who beautifies, dignifies, and crowns you with loving–kindness and tender mercy." –Psalm 103:4 (Amp)

"The Spirit of the Sovereign Lord is on me, because the Lord has anointed me to preach good news to the poor. He has sent me to bind up the brokenhearted, to proclaim freedom for the captives and release from darkness for the prisoners… and provide for those who grieve in Zion– to bestow on them a crown of beauty instead of ashes, the oil of gladness instead of mourning, and a garment of praise instead of a spirit of despair." –Isaiah 61:1,3

"The Lord redeems His servants; no one will be condemned who take refuge in Him." –Psalm 34:22

My Personal Experience:

You are the RESURRECTION and the life.

"But Christ has indeed been raised from the dead, the first fruits of those who have fallen asleep. For since death came through a man, the resurrection of the dead comes also through a man. For as in Adam all die, so in Christ all will be made alive." –1 Corinthians 15:20–22

"Praise be to the God and Father of our Lord Jesus Christ! In his great mercy he has given us new birth into a living hope through the resurrection of Jesus Christ from the dead," –1 Peter 1:3

"Jesus answered, I am the way and the truth and the life. No one comes to the Father except through me." –John 14:6

"Now this is eternal life: that they may know you, the only true God, and Jesus Christ, whom you have sent." –John 17:3

"Jesus said to her, I am the resurrection and the life. He who believes in me will live, even though he dies." –John 11:25

My Personal Experience:

You are the REFRESHING God.

"Repent, then, and turn to God, so that your sins may be wiped out, that times of refreshing may come from the Lord." –Acts 3:19

"You gave abundant showers of God, You refresh your weary inheritance." –Psalm 68:9

"He refreshes my life." –Psalm 23:3

My Personal Experience:

You are the REVIVING God.

"For this is what the high and lofty One says– He who lives forever, whose name is Holy: 'I live in a high and holy place, but also with him who is contrite and lowly in spirit, to revive the spirit of the lowly and to revive the heart of the contrite'." –Isaiah 57:15

"After two days He will revive us; on the third day He will restore us, that we may live in His presence." –Hosea 6:2

"Will you not revive us again, that Your people may rejoice in You." –Psalm 85:6

My Personal Experience:

You are the RENOWNED God.

"Yes, Lord, walking in the way of Your laws, we wait for You; Your name and renown are the desire of our hearts." –Isaiah 26:8

"The Lord God Almighty, the Lord is His name of renown!" –Hosea 12:5

"But You, O Lord, sit enthroned forever; your renown endures through all generations." –Psalm 102:12

My Personal Experience:

You are the RELENTING God.

"Then the Lord relented and did not bring on His people the disaster He had threatened." –Exodus 32:14

"Perhaps they will listen and each will turn from his evil way. Then I will relent and not bring on them the disaster I was planning because of the evil they have done." –Jeremiah 26:3

"Rend your heart and not your garments. Return to the Lord your God, for He is gracious and compassionate, slow to anger and abounding in love, and He relents from sending calamity." –Joel 2:13

"…I knew that you are a gracious and compassionate God, slow to anger and abounding in love, a God who relents from sending calamity." –Jonah 4:2

"For their sake He remembered His covenant and out of His great love He relented." –Psalm 106:45

My Personal Experience:

You are the REMEMBERING God.

"To Him Who [earnestly] remembered us in our low estate and imprinted us [on His heart], for His mercy and loving-kindness endure forever." –Psalm 136:23 (Amp)

"Then God remembered Rachel; He listened to her and opened her womb." –Genesis 30:22

"He has remembered His love and His faithfulness to the house of Israel; all the ends of the earth have seen the salvation of our God." –Psalm 98:3

"And the Lord remembered her–Hannah cried out to God." –1 Samuel 1:19

My Personal Experience:

You are the God who RECONCILES me to Yourself.

"And God purposed that through Him [the Son] all things should be completely reconciled back to Himself, whether on earth or in heaven..." –Colossians 1:20 (Amp)

"Yet now has [Christ, the Messiah] reconciled [you to God] in the body of His flesh through death, in order to present you holy and faultless and irreproachable in His [the Father's] presence." –Colossians 1:22 (Amp)

"God reconciled men to Himself." –2 Corinthians 5:19

My Personal Experience:

You are the RADIANT God.

"And the city has no need of the sun nor of the moon to give light to it, for the splendor and radiance (glory) of God illuminate it, and the Lamb is its lamp." –Revelation 21:23

"Those who look to him are radiant; their faces are never covered with shame." –Psalm 34:5

"My lover is radiant and ruddy, outstanding among ten thousand." –Song of Solomon 5:10

"And I saw the glory of the God of Israel coming from the east. His voice was like the roar of rushing waters, and the land was radiant with his glory." –Ezekiel 43:2

"His radiance is like the sunshine." –Habakkuk 3:4

My Personal Experience:

You are the RENEWER of my strength.

"Who satisfies your desires with good things so that your youth is renewed like the eagle's." –Psalm 103:5

"He will renew your life and sustain you in your old age..." –Ruth 4:15

"Create in me a clean heart, O God, and renew a steadfast spirit within me." –Psalm 51:10 (NASB)

"But those who hope in the Lord renew their strength." –Isaiah 40:31

My Personal Experience:

You are the RESTORING God.

"So I will restore to you the years that the swarming locusts has eaten..." - Joel 2:25

"Restore us, O God; make your face shine upon us, that we may be saved." -Psalm 80:3

"He restores my soul..." -Psalm 23:3

My Personal Experience:

You are my STRONGHOLD, and SAFE PLACE.

"My God, my Rock, in Him will I take refuge; my Shield and the Horn of my salvation; my Stronghold and my Refuge, my Savior–You save me from violence." –2 Samuel 22:3 (Amp)

"My people shall dwell in a peaceable habitation, in safe dwellings, and in quiet resting–places." –Isaiah 32:18 (Amp)

"You are a stronghold in times of trouble." –Psalm 9:9

My Personal Experience:

You are my SHIELD.

"After these things, the word of the Lord came to Abram in a vision, saying, Fear not, Abram, I am your Shield, your abundant compensation, and your reward shall be exceedingly great." –Genesis 15:1 (Amp)

"My God, my Rock, in Him will I take refuge; my Shield and the Horn of my salvation; my Stronghold and my Refuge, my Savior–You save me from violence." –2 Samuel 22:3 (Amp)

"You are a shield around me O Lord." –Psalm 3:3

My Personal Experience:

You are the SURROUNDING God.

"You are a hiding place for me; You, Lord, preserve me from trouble, You surround me with songs and shouts of deliverance." –Psalm 32:7 (Amp)

"You surround Your righteous with your favor as a shield." –Psalm 5:12

My Personal Experience:

You are the God who SHOWS me Your ways.

"Now the Lord said to Abram, Go for yourself away from your country, from your relatives and your father's house, to the land that I will show you." –Genesis 12:1 (Amp)

"But for this very purpose have I let you live, that I might show you My power, and that My name may be declared throughout all the earth." –Exodus 9:16 (Amp)

"…He guides me in paths of righteousness for His name's sake." –Psalm 23:3

"Show me your ways O Lord teach me Your paths." –Psalm 25:4

My Personal Experience:

You are my SAVIOR.

"For I am the Lord your God, the Holy One of Israel, your Savior;" –Isaiah 43:3 (Amp)

"He is a Savior and Deliverer, and He works signs and wonders in the heavens and on the earth––He Who has delivered Daniel from the power of the lions." –Daniel 6:27 (Amp)

"The Lord your God is in the midst of you, a Mighty One, a Savior. He will rejoice over you with joy… " –Zephaniah 3:17 (Amp)

"He will call out to me, 'You are my Father, my God, the Rock my Savior.'" –Psalm 89:26

My Personal Experience: _____

_____

You are the God who SENDS help.

"He sends forth His word and heals them and rescues them from the pit and destruction." –Psalm 107:20 (Amp)

"May He send you help from the sanctuary and grant you support from Zion." –Psalm 20:2

My Personal Experience: _____

_____

You are my SHEPHERD.

"For the Lamb at the center of the throne will be their shepherd; He will lead them to springs of living water. And God will wipe away every tear from their eyes." –Revelation 7:17

"I have other sheep that are not of this sheep pen. I must bring them also. They too will listen to my voice, and there shall be one flock and one shepherd." –John 10:16

"The Lord is my Shepherd, I shall not be in want." –Psalm 23:1

My Personal Experience: _____

_____

You are the God who STILLS my hunger.

"For He satisfies the thirsty and fills the hungry with good things." –Psalm 107:9

"You still the hunger of those You cherish, their sons have plenty and they store up wealth for their own children." –Psalm 17:14

My Personal Experience: _____

_____

You are my STRENGTH.

"The Lord is good, a Strength and Stronghold in the day of trouble…" –Nahum 1:7 (Amp)

"Unto You, O my Strength, I will sing praises; for God is my Defense, my Fortress, and High Tower, the God Who shows me mercy and steadfast love." –Psalm 59:17 (Amp)

"My flesh and my heart may fail, but God is the Rock and firm Strength of my heart and my Portion forever." –Psalm 71:26 (Amp)

"The Lord is my strength and my shield, my heart trust in Him and I am helped, my heart leaps for joy." –Psalm 29:7

My Personal Experience: _____

_____

You are the SUSTAINER God.

"For forty years you sustained them in the desert; they lacked nothing, their clothes did not wear out nor did their feet become swollen." –Nehemiah 9:21

"I lie down and sleep; I wake again, because the Lord sustains me." –Psalm 3:5

"You give me Your shield of victory, and Your right hand sustains me; You stoop down to make me great." –Psalm 18:35

"Surely God is my help, the Lord is the one who sustains me." –Psalm 54:4

My Personal Experience:

You are the SAVING God.

"The Lord your God is in the midst of you, a Mighty One, a Savior [Who saves]!" –Zephaniah 3:17 (Amp)

"My defense and shield depend on God, Who saves the upright in heart." –Psalm 7:10 (Amp)

"He sends from heaven and saves me, rebuking those who pursue me." –Psalm 57:3

My Personal Experience:

You are the SPLITTER of the rock

"He split the rocks in the desert and gave them water as abundant as the seas."-Psalm 78:15

My Personal Experience:

You are the STRONG TOWER.

"For You have been a shelter and a refuge for me, a strong tower against the adversary." –Psalm 61:3 (Amp)

"The name of the Lord is a strong tower, the righteous run to it and are safe." –Proverbs 18:10

My Personal Experience:

You are the SUN AND SHIELD to those You love.

"The sun will no more be your light by day, nor will the brightness of the moon shine on you, for the Lord will be your everlasting light, and your God will be your glory." –Isaiah 60:19

"But for you who revere my name, the sun of righteousness will rise with healing in its wings. And you will go out and leap like calves released from the stall." –Malachi 4:2

"For the Lord God is a sun and a shield; the Lord bestows favor and honor. No thing does He withhold from those whose walk is blameless." –Psalm 84:11

My Personal Experience:

You are the SATISFYING God.

"For He satisfies the longing soul and fills the hungry soul with good."–Psalm 107:9 (Amp)

"As for me, I will continue beholding Your face in; I shall be fully satisfied, when I awake beholding Your form." –Psalm 17:15 (Amp)

"You satisfy us in the morning with you unfailing love." –Psalm 90:14

"With long life will I satisfy him and show him my salvation." –Psalm 92:16

My Personal Experience:

You are the SUPPORTING God.

"They confronted me in the day of my disaster, but the Lord was my support." –2 Samuel 22:19

"May He send you help from the sanctuary and grant you support from Zion." –Psalm 20:2

"When I said, 'my foot is slipping, Your love O Lord supported me; when anxiety was great within me, Your consolation brought joy to my soul." –Psalm 94:18

My Personal Experience:

You are the God who STILLS the storm.

"Without warning, a furious storm came up on the lake, so that the waves swept over the boat. But Jesus was sleeping… Then He got up and rebuked the winds and the waves, and it was completely calm." –Matthew 8: 24,26

"He stilled the storm to a whisper; the waves of the sea were hushed. They were glad when it grew calm and He guided them to their desired haven." –Psalm 107:29

My Personal Experience:

You are SLOW to anger.

"…He is gracious and compassionate, slow to anger and abounding in love, and He relents from sending calamity." –Joel 2:13

"The Lord is slow to anger and great in power; the Lord will not leave the guilty unpunished. His way is in the whirlwind and the storm, and clouds are the dust of his feet." –Nahum 1:3

"The Lord is not slow in keeping His promises." –2 Peter 3:9

"The Lord, the compassionate and gracious God, slow to anger, abounding in love and faithfulness." –Exodus 34:6

My Personal Experience:

You are the SERVANT God.

"Listen, O high priest Joshua and your associates seated before you, who are men symbolic of things to come: I am going to bring my servant, the Branch." –Zechariah 3:8

"The God of Abraham, Isaac and Jacob, the God of our fathers, has glorified His servant Jesus..." –Acts 3:13

"Stretch out your hand to heal and perform miraculous signs and wonders through the name of your holy servant Jesus." –Acts 4:30

"Here is my servant, whom I uphold, my chosen one in whom I delight; I will put my Spirit on him and he will bring justice to the nations." –Isaiah 21:1

My Personal Experience:

You are my SURE FOUNDATION.

"He will be the sure foundation for your times, a rich store of salvation and wisdom and knowledge; the fear of the Lord is the key to this treasure." –Isaiah 33:6

"For no one can lay any foundation other than the one already laid, which is Jesus Christ." –1 Corinthians 3:11

"So this is what the Sovereign Lord says: See, I lay a stone in Zion, a tested stone, a precious cornerstone for a sure foundation; the one who trusts will never be dismayed." –Isaiah 28:16

My Personal Experience:

You are my SUPPLIER.

"And my God shall supply all your need according to His riches in glory by Christ Jesus." –Philippians 4:19 (NKJV)

"Now may He who supplies seed to the sower, and bread for food, supply and multiply the seed you have sown and increase the fruits of your righteousness," –2 Corinthians 9:10 (NKJV))

My Personal Experience:

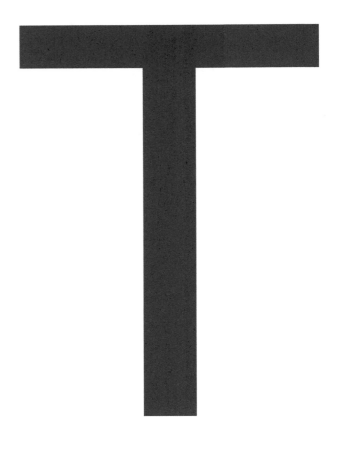

You are the TRAINING God.

"And He trains each of them correctly for his God instructs Him correctly and teaches him. "–Isaiah 28:26 (Amp)

"He trains my hands for war, so that my arms can bend a bow of bronze." –2 Samuel 22:35 (Amp)

"He trains my hands for battle and makes my way perfect." –Psalm 18:32

My Personal Experience:

You are the TEACHER.

"…For you have one Teacher, the Christ." –Matthew 23:10

"And after she had said this, she went back and called her sister Mary aside. 'The Teacher is here,' she said, 'and is asking for you.'" –John 11:28

"You call me 'Teacher' and 'Lord,' and rightly so, for that is what I am." –John 13:13

"Show me Your ways O Lord, teach me Your path guide me in Your truth and teach me." –Psalm 25:4

My Personal Experience:

You are the TRUSTWORTHY God.

"As for God, His way is perfect; the word of the Lord is tried. He is a Shield to all those who trust and take refuge in Him." –2 Samuel 22:31 (Amp)

"I will say of the Lord, 'He is my refuge and my fortress. My God, in whom I trust." –Palm 91:2

"You are God, Your words are trustworthy." –2 Samuel 7:28

"All Your commands are trustworthy." –Psalm 119:86

My Personal Experience:

You are the God who THINKS of me.

"Many, O Lord my God, are the wonderful works which You have done, and Your thoughts toward us; no one can compare with You!" –Psalm 40:5 (Amp)

"How precious to me are Your thoughts, O God. How vast is the sum of them." –Psalm 139:17

"Lord, what is man that You care for him, the son of man that You think of him?" –Psalm 144:3

My Personal Experience:

You are the TALKING God who desires to talk to me.

"Gideon said to Him, If now I have found favor in Your sight, then show me a sign that it is You Who talks with me." –Judges 6:17 (Amp)

"The attendants replied, 'Never has a man talked as this Man talks!" –John 7:46 (Amp)

"Call to me and I will answer you and tell you great and unsearchable things you do not know." –Jeremiah 33:3

My Personal Experience: _____

_____

You are the TRIUMPHANT God.

"Then Moses and the Israelites sang this song to the Lord, saying, I will sing to the Lord, for He has triumphed gloriously…"
–Exodus 15:1. (Amp)

"…My heart exults and triumphs in the Lord; my horn (my strength) is lifted up in the Lord. My mouth is no longer silent, for it
  is opened wide over my enemies, because I rejoice in Your salvation." –1 Samuel 2:1 (Amp)

"The Lord will march out like a mighty man, like a warrior. He will stir up His zeal and He will triumph over His enemies." –Isaiah 42:13

"He made a public spectacle of them triumphing over them by the cross." –Colossians 2:15

My Personal Experience: _____

You are the TRUTHFUL God.

"But the Lord is the true God and the God of truth." –Jeremiah 10:10 (Amp)

"But when the Comforter comes, Whom I will send to you from the Father, the Spirit of Truth Who comes from the Father, He
  [Himself] will testify regarding Me." –John 15:26 (Amp)

"God is not a man, that He should lie, nor a son of man, that He should change His mind. Does He speak and then not act?
  Does He promise and not fulfill?" –Numbers 23:19

"He who is the Glory of Israel does not lie or change His mind; for He is not a man, that He should change His mind." –1 Samuel 15:29

"Jesus answered them, I am the way and the truth and the life." –John 14:6

"A faith and knowledge resting on the hope of eternal life, which God, who cannot lie, promised before the world began." –Titus 1:2

My Personal Experience: _____

You are the God who calls me your TREASURED possession

"…To be His people, His treasured possession." - Deuteronomy 7:6

"…You will be my treasured possession…" -Exodus 19:5

My Personal Experience: _____

You are the TRUE VINE.

"I am the true vine, and my Father is the gardener." -John 15:1

My Personal Experience: _____

You are the UPHOLDING God

"For you have upheld my right and my cause…" -Psalm 9:4

"The Lord upholds all those who fall and lifts up all who are bowed down, the eyes of all who look to You and You give them their food at the proper time." -Psalm 145:14-15

"He upholds the cause of the oppressed and gives food to the hungry…" -Psalm 146:7

"I am the Lord, Your God, who upholds your right hand."- Isaiah 41:13

My Personal Experience:

You are the UPRIGHT God.

"Righteous are You, O Lord, and upright are Your judgments and all expressions of Your will." –Psalm 119:137 (Amp)

"Upright and just is He!" –Deuteronomy 32:4

"Good and upright is the Lord." –Psalm 25:8

"Upright One, You make a way of the righteous smooth." –Isaiah 26:7

My Personal Experience:

You are the UNCHANGING God.

"Who has prepared and done this, calling forth and guiding the destinies of the generations [of the nations] from the beginning? I, the Lord––the first and with the last [an ever–present, unchanging God – I am He." –Isaiah 41:4 (Amp)

My Personal Experience:

You are the UNDERSTANDING God.

"And God, who is acquainted with and understands the heart, bore witness to them, giving them the Holy Spirit as He also did to us…" –Acts 15:8 (Amp)

"To God belong wisdom and power; counsel and understanding are His." –Job 12:13

"Great is our Lord and mighty in power; His understanding has no limit." –Psalm 147:5

"And how from your childhood you have had a knowledge of and been acquainted with the sacred writings, which are able to instruct you and give you the understanding for salvation which comes through faith in Christ Jesus." –2 Timothy 3:15 (Amp)

"I gain understanding from your precepts; therefore I hate every wrong path." –Psalm 119:104

My Personal Experience:

You are the UNCREATED God

"In the beginning God created the heavens and the earth." - Genesis 1:1

"In the beginning was the Word and the Word was with God and the Word was God." - John 1:1

My Personal Experience:

_____

You are the UNFAILING God

"Have mercy on me O God; according to Your unfailing love, according to your great compassion, blot out my transgressions." -Psalm 51:1

"...The earth is full of His unfailing love." -Psalm 33:5

"...I trust in God's unfailing love forever and ever." - Psalm 52:8

"Satisfy us in the morning with Your unfailing love..." - Psalm 90:14

My Personal Experience:

_____

_____

You are the UNSPEAKABLE GIFT

"Thanks be to God for his unspeakable gift!" -2 Corinthians 9:15 (ASV)

My Personal Experience:

_____

_____

You are the VINDICATING God.

"Vindicate me, O Lord, for I have walked in my integrity; I have trusted in, leaned on, and relied on the Lord without wavering and I shall not slide." –Psalm 26:1 (Amp)

"Save me, O God, by Your name; judge and vindicate me by Your mighty strength and power." –Psalm 54:1 (Amp)

"May my vindication come from You..." –Psalm 17:2

"Vindicate me in Your righteousness O Lord my God, do not let them gloat over me." –Psalm 35:24

My Personal Experience:

You are the VICTORIOUS God.

"The Lord your God is in your midst, a victorious warrior He will exult over you with joy, He will be quiet in His love, He will rejoice over you with shouts of joy." –Zephaniah 3:17 (NASB)

"Yet I will rejoice in the Lord; I will exult in the [victorious] God of my salvation!" –Habakkuk 3:18 (Amp

"In Your majesty ride forth victoriously in behalf of truth, humility and righteousness." –Psalm 45:4

"He will swallow up death in victory." –Isaiah 25:8

My Personal Experience:

You are the VOICEFUL God.

"The voice of the Lord is over the waters; the God of glory thunders, the Lord thunders over the mighty waters. The voice of the Lord is powerful; the voice of the Lord is majestic. The voice of the Lord breaks the cedars; the Lord breaks in pieces the cedars of Lebanon... The voice of the Lord strikes with flashes of lightning. The voice of the Lord shakes the desert; the Lord shakes the Desert of Kadesh. The voice of the Lord twists the oaks and strips the forests bare. And in his temple all cry, Glory!" –Psalm 29:3–9

"[Hark!] An uproar from the city! A voice from the temple! The voice of the Lord, rendering recompense to His enemies!" –Isaiah 66:6 (Amp)

"The voice of the Lord is powerful, the voice of the Lord is majestic." –Psalm 9:4

My Personal Experience:

You are the VINE.

"I am the True Vine, and My Father is the Vinedresser." –John 15:1

"Remain in me, and I will remain in you. No branch can bear fruit by itself; it must remain in the vine. Neither can you bear fruit unless you remain in me. I am the vine; you are the branches. If a man remains in me and I in him, he will bear much fruit; apart from Me you can do nothing." –John 15:4–5

My Personal Experience:

You are the WORKING God.

"Hear this, O Job; stand still and consider the wondrous works of God." –Job 37:14 (Amp)

"Many, O Lord my God, are the wonderful works which You have done, and Your thoughts toward us; no one can compare with You! If I should declare and speak of them, they are too many to be numbered." –Psalm 40:5 (Amp)

"And we know that in all things God works for the good of those who love Him, who have been called according to His purposes." –Romans 8:28

My Personal Experience:

You are WITH me.

"And the Lord appeared to him the same night and said, 'I am the God of Abraham your father. Fear not, for I am with you and will favor you with blessings and multiply your descendants for the sake of My servant Abraham'." –Genesis 26:24 (Amp)

"Be strong, courageous, and firm; fear not nor be in terror before them, for it is the Lord your God Who goes with you; He will not fail you or forsake you." –Deuteronomy 31:6 (Amp)

"…And surely I am with you always, to the very end of the age." –Matthew 28:20

"I fear no evil for you are with me." –Psalm 23:4

"The Lord Almighty is with us, the God of Jacob is our fortress." –Psalm 46:7

"And they said, we saw certainly that the Lord was with us." –Genesis 26:28

My Personal Experience:

You are the WATCHFUL God.

"We know that anyone born of God does not practice committing sin, but the One Who was begotten of God carefully watches over and protects him, and the wicked one does not lay hold on him or touch [him]." –1 John 5:18 (Amp)

"He will not let your foot slip; He who watches over you will not slumber, indeed He who watches over Israel will neither slumber nor sleep. The Lord watches over you; The Lord is your shade at your right hand; the sun will not harm you by day, not the moon by night. The Lord will keep you from all harm; he will watch over your life; the Lord will watch over your coming and going, both now and forevermore." –Psalm 121:3-8

My Personal Experience:

You are the WAY.

"He is the Rock, His work is perfect, for all His ways are law and justice. A God of faithfulness without breach or deviation, just and right is He." –Deuteronomy 32:4 (Amp)

"As for God, His way is perfect; the word of the Lord is tried. He is a Shield to all those who trust and take refuge in Him." –2 Samuel 22:31 (Amp)

"As for God, His way is perfect!" –Psalm 18:30 (Amp)

"The ways of the Lord are right." –Hosea 14:9

"Your ways, O God are holy." –Psalm 77:13

My Personal Experience:

You are the WISE God.

"[God] is wise in heart and mighty in strength…" –Job 9:4

"…God is wiser than men, and the weak thing from God is stronger than men." –1 Corinthians 1:25 (Amp)

"By wisdom the Lord laid the earth's foundations, by understanding He set the heavens in place;" –Proverbs 3:19

"He founded the world by His wisdom" –Jeremiah 10:12

My Personal Experience:

You are the God who WITHHOLDS no good thing from those You love.

"For the Lord God is a sun and shield; the Lord bestows favor and honor; no good thing does He withhold from those whose walk is blameless." –Psalm 84:11

"You gave your good Spirit to instruct them. You did not withhold Your manna from their mouths, and You gave them water for their thirst." –Nehemiah 9:20

"You, O Lord, will not withhold Your compassion from me; Your loving–kindness and Your truth will continually preserve me." –Psalm 40:11 (NASB)

"No good thing does He withhold." –Psalm 84:11

My Personal Experience:

You are the WITNESS.

"The elders of Gilead replied, "The Lord is our witness; we will certainly do as you say." –Judges 11:10

"Even now my witness is in heaven; my advocate is on high." –Job 16:19

"See, I have made him a witness to the peoples" –Isaiah 55:4

My Personal Experience:

You are the WORD.

"In the beginning was the Word, and the Word was with God, and the Word was God." –John 1:1

"The Word became flesh and made His dwelling among us. We have seen His glory, the glory of the One and Only, who came from the Father, full of grace and truth." –John 1:14

"The Word of the Lord is flawless." –2 Samuel 22:31

"Your Word is a lamp unto my feet." –Psalm 119:105

My Personal Experience:

You are WONDERFUL God.

"...Your love for me is wonderful..." - 2 Samuel 1:26

"...For He showed His wonderful love to me..."- Psalm 31:21

"Your statutes are wonderful..." -Psalm 119:21

"....Your works are wonderful.." -Psalm 139:14

"...Wonderful Counselor, Mighty God..." -Isaiah 9:6

My Personal Experience:

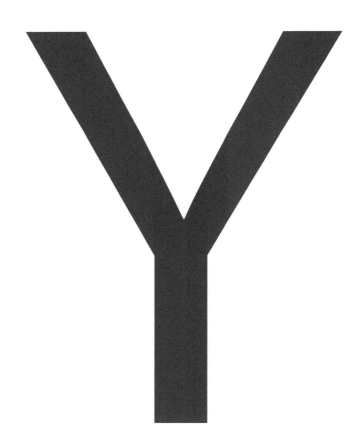

You are YAHWEH.

"...My name the Lord [Yahweh––the redemptive name of God]..." –Exodus 6:3

"And God said to Moses, 'I am Yahweh – the Lord." –Exodus 6:2 (NLT)

"The Lord is a warrior; Yahweh is His name!" –Exodus 15:13 (NLT)

"Let them know you, whose name is Yahweh, that You alone are the Most High over all the earth." –Psalm 83:18

My Personal Experience:

You are the easy YOKE.

"Take my yoke upon you and learn from me, for I am gentle and humble in heart, and you will find rest for your souls."
–Matthew 11:29

"...You have shattered the yoke that burdens them, the bar across their shoulders, the rod of their oppressor." –Isaiah 9:4

"Is not this the kind of fasting I have chosen: to loose the chains of injustice and untie the cords of the yoke, to set the oppressed free and break every yoke?" –Isaiah 58:6

"I led them with cords of human kindness, with ties of love; I lifted the yoke from their neck and bent down to feed them."
–Hosea 11:4

"It is for freedom that Christ has set us free. Stand firm, then, and do not let yourselves be burdened again by a yoke of slavery." –Galatians 5:1

"For my yoke is easy and my burden is light." –Matthew 11:30

My Personal Experience:

You the same YESTERDAY, today, and forever.

"Jesus Christ is the same yesterday, and today, and forever." –Hebrews 13:8

My Personal Experience:

You are the God who is ZEALOUS.

"For out of Jerusalem shall go forth a remnant, and a band of survivors out of Mount Zion. The zeal of the Lord of hosts shall perform this." –2 Kings 19:31 (Amp)

"His disciples remembered that it is written: 'Zeal for your house will consume me.'" –John 2:17

"My zeal has consumed me." –Psalm 119:39

"...He will arouse His zeal like a man of war..." –Isaiah 42:13

"...The zeal of the Lord will perform the promises made." –Isaiah 9:7

My Personal Experience:

You are the God who is enthroned on ZION.

"I have installed My King on Zion, My holy hill." –Psalm 2:6

"Sing praises to the Lord, enthroned in Zion; proclaim among the nations what He has done." –Psalm 9:11

"It is beautiful in its loftiness, the joy of the whole earth. Like the utmost heights of Zaphon is Mount Zion, the city of the Great King." –Psalm 48:2

"From Zion, perfect in beauty, God shines forth." –Psalm 50:2

"Great is the Lord in Zion; He is exalted over all the nations." –Psalm 99:2

"Then I looked, and there before me was the Lamb, standing on Mount Zion, and with Him 144,000 who had His name and his Father's name written on their foreheads." –Revelation 14:1

My Personal Experience:

For more on
Adoration resources:

Hope Broadcast
Join us weekly for our Hope Broadcast with Bob Hartley and Bob Fraser, a prophetic, hope filled message to the Body of Christ which is viewable on our website, BobHartley.org.

52 Weeks
New for this year, in just 20 minutes per week Bob Hartley mentors you in how to practically live a lifestyle of Hope in every arena of life. Each weekly lesson is short and practical. Develop an ability to Hear God that will transfer into your family, business and personal life. Sign up today at 52weeksofhope.com.

Prayer CD's & Podcast
The Prayer Podcast features our team modeling for you how to adore and inquire of the heart of the Lord in your everyday life. The prayer CD's model how to encounter the different faces or characteristics of God as a Builder, Supplier, Redeemer and Wise God (*Visit our archived podcasts at bobhartley.org)

Morning Marketplace Prayer Conference Call
Call in every 9 am CST M-F as we adore and proclaim together the 4 faces of God for Organizations and Business. (Builder, Redeemer, Supplier, and Wise God).
   • Conf. # 218-339-0361 code: hope#

Further Training
Contact our team at: hopeorders@gmail.com about our Hartley Institute Mentoring program:

   Two Day Presence Based Conference/ Workshops & Quarterly Events
   •   Learn the value of Jesus in your business or organization
   •   Learn to hear God's voice for you and your business or organization
   •   Learn to invite God into the decision making process
   •   Monthly mentoring for Organizations and Businesses

For more information on resources at Bobhartley.org